Oxbow Lake

Oxbow Lake

Eileen Lao

Translated from the Chinese by
Samuel Singler, Eileen Lao

AcerBooks

Oxbow Lake (Acer Novels Book 1)
Author: Eileen Lao
English translation: Samuel Singler, Eileen Lao
Cover painting: Eileen Lao
Design: Tao Zhijian

ISBN: 978-1-0688485-2-0

Publisher: Acer Books Canada, International Humanities Publishers, Montreal, Canada
Email: acerbookscanada@gmail.com

Acer Novels (Series)
Plan and Design: Tao Zhijian

Contents

Homesick

Homesickness
It is a poem
It is a mumbling song
A little bird draped in colorful clothes
That awakens
The silent dawn
Is it a ray of sunlight
That urges on
The tardy spring
Is it the tulips of May
Gorgeous and vibrant, yet nearing their end

I brew a pot of Yunnan Pu'er tea
Not forgetting
To brew another cup of French coffee.

Outside the window
Is a river named
Rivière-des-Mille-Îles
Flowing through the Thousand Islands.

Abstract

"Oxbow Lake" tells the story of a generation, Generation W. I am the one who coined this term.

My parents' generation, I call it Generation W. W stands for War, W stands for Water, W represents the generation before Generations X, Y, and Z. W is also a professional symbol in geology, representing an oxbow lake.

Even to this day, as it has been for hundreds of years, the Chinese still find it necessary to depart their hometown. They carry heavy burdens and wander around continuously, as if searching for a better life, with the hope of one day returning home in full glory. But everyone gets physically and mentally exhausted eventually, and when they are tired, they could no longer wander, just like my parents, who ultimately stayed in a foreign land.

A person's life is like an oxbow lake.

As I decided to write a book, I interviewed many people who were friends of my parents. I put together all the stories I heard from them with the bits and pieces my parents told me when they were still alive and turned all of it into an "epic."

Many details in this book are only touched upon briefly, and the events of those years are pieced together from scattered information. The stories in this book are not only about my family's history.

In this book, *Oxbow Lake*, I've included four stories and two short poems, all based on real-life histories. Life has so many unexpected turns that I do not need to rely on imagination to write a book.

Every generation's life must undergo trials. My parents lived in a time of war, and surviving well took all their efforts in life, as is described in "Thunder from the South of the Cloud."

Most of our generation of Chinese people have not experienced war firsthand, or not yet, but our generation has gone through tremendous changes. The hardships we face are more emotional, and everyone feels lonely, like Fei in "Don't Be too Sentimental" and "Don't Go Further", which are the same story told twice, from a woman's as well as a man's perspectives.

Oxbow Lake

1. Generation W

"THOSE WHO GET to live in Canada surely are being looked after from above."

I feel so grateful that I could come to live in Canada. I don't know much about the guardian angel that took such a special interest in me, but I know now that he had a hand in leading me here. I know there is but one God, and that he is surrounded by many angels. I also know that everyone God cares for has its own guardian angel. The guardian angel that follows me, I can really feel his presence. I can tell he is a "he" rather than a "she". He even once broke the rule that forbids them to show themselves, to rescue me in a most perilous moment.

But does God only live in Canada? Are the Angels only in Canada? What about my childhood? What about my youth? Looking back, I doubt that there was an angel by my side during that time. Maybe there was, but I have forgotten, just as I have forgotten most of the things that happened when I was young.

I wonder today, how did my childhood go? How about my teenage years? and thereafter? Can I say that my life was an ordinary one? The answer to these questions is still elusive. Maybe the answer awaits my parting from this world to reveal itself to my sons, who will be the ultimate judges of it. I know however that, at least compared to those who have achieved wonders and led brilliant lives, my own experience is not worth mentioning. Even so, I still feel that I am “uncommon”. I am like a small stream of water, I flow through mountains, through oceans, through cities, and through countries. I flow quietly and humbly. Isn’t that unstopping flow not worth a mention? Isn’t that a strength in itself, something to be proud of?

I really regret today to have not listened enough to my parents while they were still alive. I wish I would have listened more to what they had to say, I could have taken notes and recorded their life’s story. It was only later, after they had both passed away, when my own children asked me about them, that I began to think about my parent’s lives. I eventually decided to write down the memories of my parents using fragments of souvenirs from others who knew them. I didn’t intend to do this to share it or to present it to anyone, but my sole purpose was to find answers to my questions and put my mind to rest.

Isn't this a regret in the heart of all sons and daughters? While our parents are alive, we always lack the time, we're never in the mood for their stories. We could almost say that we simply do not bother listening to them telling their life's stories. In our young eyes, our parents are just two boring elderly persons staying at home, who always want to discuss uninteresting topics at inappropriate times. They are out of date, they can't keep up with the rhythm of our time, and their past is irrelevant to our reality, we see it as having nothing to do with us. We will pay attention, however, to strangers, people entirely unrelated to us, such as movie stars, athletes, or political figures, but won't show even a bit of interest in our parents. Until one day they leave the world, leaving us behind. We then slowly start to miss them. We begin to regret our past behavior, the coldness, the indifference. And then one day, we may hear about our parents from other people. Seeing other people's admiration and praise for our parents, we then "wake up" and begin to seek their stories.

We refer to people who were born from the 1960s to the 1980s as Generation X, and those born in the mid-1980s to 2000 as Generation Y, and those born after 2000 as Generation Z.

So, could the generation of my parents be called Generation W? W standing for War, and for Water. In those days, they experienced two world wars and my parents' lives resembled much running water, a water that's always flowing around. Water on the move is always looking for the ocean, for a safe place to stay.

Before the Generations X, Y, and Z, was Generation W, and it's a generation just like all the others.

2. Go Foreign

Perhaps out of nostalgia for the ponytail his father had, when my grandfather left China for Indonesia, he decided to grow a beard. Over the course of years, his beard gradually grew ever longer. Its color eventually turned from pitch-black to snow-white, as his sturdy character was softening. My grandfather often told stories to his grandchildren under the shade of a big tree. Because of his surname Yang, Grandpa's favorite story was "Generals of the Yang Family" based on the story of the Yangs during the Song dynasty. He also liked to tell the famous Chinese story "Romance of the Three Kingdoms". When Grandpa was telling his stories, kids silently sat around him, this was his happiest time. Grandpa had a hearty laugh and when he was laughing, his long beard bent into the shape of a lunar crescent. Grandpa had a scholarly look, he wore a pair of round glasses like those that Puyi, the last Chinese Emperor of the Qing Dynasty, used to wear. He looked like the kind of well-cultivated pedant professor that can be found in old schools. Everyone in the village had great respect for him, even those Japanese soldiers who were stationed there, along with their respective families.

My grandfather, through his stories to children, had always presented the Japanese as being very polite, and law-abiding. These children would later discover, having reached adult age, the atrocities that the Japanese had committed against the Chinese people during the war. The people in Indonesia had seen the Japanese torture and murder the Dutch. It was hard for them to understand Grandpa's point of view on the Japanese. Some figured he must have been just another "coolie", "sold" to work the land in south-east Asia. Without any education, they thought his opinion was naturally biased, so they stopped paying him attention on this matter.

I never thought that I had grandparents. Of course, everyone has grandparents. If there are parents, there must be grandparents. What I want to say is that when I began looking for the history of my parents, I did not think that the story would start from my grandparents, more specifically my mother's parents. No matter how far I look back in time, I have no recollections of them whatsoever.

My investigation started with my brother who lived close to me in Montreal. He is the second son of the family, my only relative in Canada. My other two brothers and one sister did not immigrate to Canada, neither the older brother nor the sister were qualified for immigration. My third brother once thought about immigrating, so he submitted the application and got an official interview. However, when the immigration officer asked him why he wanted to immigrate to Canada, instead of giving the standard answer that could get you a quick and easy approval such as "I like Canada's peacefulness", or any other compliment of the country of that kind, my casual brother's answer was: "I am not overly excited about immigrating, if you allow me, I will come, but if you do not, it's really no big deal." What was the reaction of the Canadian officer? Of course it was "no big deal", his application was rejected.

The cities Haifeng and Lufeng, together called Hailufeng, are both located close to water and mountains, with the rich resources that surround them, they should not have been as poor as they were, but even today, my hometown has never really improved its situation. Departing from Shenzhen and Guangzhou, two of the richest cities in China, a car drive takes just about two hours to reach this region. When the bus arrives at Shanwei, a small town in the area, you can immediately feel the "desolation". The dialect is different, customs are not the same, the economy is under-developed, the people staunchly stick to their own local set of traditional rules. As soon as you get there, you feel like you've just been taken 20 years back.

During the Qing Dynasty, Hailufeng suffered from both natural disasters and lawlessness, and people there lived in poverty. Young men wanted to leave their hometown to make a better living abroad. It was called to "Go Foreign". A tiny minority went to North America, and most chose the southeast Asian countries, like Indonesia and Thailand. At the time, these countries were richer than China.

It takes courage to "go foreign", you need a tough character. "The Thunder God is in the sky, the people are in Hailufeng", is a Chinese saying that compares the furious thunder to the Hailufeng people, is this saying a praise or a derogation? The fact is that Hailufeng's men are brave and courageous, they fear not hardships, and wherever they live, they live together as a family. Those who have "gone foreign", will eventually return home after a few years of hard work. When they do, they come back enriched and they are very generous with the people of their township, envy is inevitably aroused in the village, which drives another flock of young men to act and "go foreign" too.

My young grandfather chose to work in a tobacco field in Indonesia with several villagers from his village, with whom he got along well. They signed a three-year contract through a middleman. For the first three years, they had to pay the middlemen's commission, which was almost all their wages. Their work shifts were long, and the work was dirty and exhausting, they were "coolies". They could only keep a small portion of their pay, but at least, the lodging and food were free. The "go foreign" people usually saved a big part of their wages, at least the part that wasn't spent gambling or that wasn't used to pay for prostitutes, and after three years of servitude, they could earn the right to stay in the country. If they opted to stay, their fate would progressively change, their conditions would improve. This new life was always better than staying in their poor Chinese hometown, so most men chose to stay, never to look back.

3. Oxbow Lake

Have you ever seen an Oxbow Lake? Most likely, you have seen one, but you just don't know that lakes of that shape are called oxbow lakes. You probably do not know either how they are formed. You all the same would not know that the water of these lakes, before forming a lake, has travelled great distances through many rivers. Upon reaching flatlands, this tired water slows down its flow, and in doing so begins to take a curved and sinuous shape, much like a long stretch of several giant adjoined W characters. Wherever this calm water flows, it takes along with it sand and mud and the longer it flows, the more it increases its burden, rendering its way forward ever more difficult. A portion of the water will resist this slowing down, and hoping to reach the ocean quicker, will summon its last forces to make a dash forward and break the bend. What will then happen to the water that remains behind? Most of it will find its way forward on the sinuous curve impossible and forming the shape of a wooden yoke tied to the neck of an ox, will remain there stagnant, forming what is called an oxbow lake. The water that succeeded in flowing over the bend, not long later, will meet the same fate as the water that was previously left behind. Eventually, it will have to stop, and never losing its longing for the sea, will turn too, into an oxbow lake.

Every day at dusk, after finishing another coolie's hard day of work on this Indonesian tobacco farm, my grandfather would usually climb up the same big tree, half-lying, and imagining the distance toward the north. He did not know in which specific direction his hometown was, but he somehow felt that the north must have been it. My 18-years old grandfather missed his parents and family, his hometown friends, but also a girl from his village named "Xian". Of course, he was not able to see his hometown from the tree. From there he could only see a succession of strange lakes, big and small. He was deeply attracted by these lakes. Even if he could not see his hometown, he would still climb up to the tree every day. For him, climbing this tree was a solemn ritual, a ritual that increased his resolve and ability to keep plowing day after day.

In a way, the fate of the oxbow lake-forming running water is somewhat like the fate of human beings. After having endured three years as a hard-working coolie, Grandfather had finally paid off all the funds borrowed from the "Coolie Broke" whom they called "Snakehead". He had borrowed from the broker to cover the cost of travelling to Indonesia but also to leave something for his parents on the day he left. Grandfather was finally a free man. Paying off the debts however was not the end, but the beginning for these young men who had left everything behind in exchange for a life of hardship. At that point, unless they suffered from serious illness, or had any other more important reason, most would choose to remain in Indonesia, unwilling to quit halfway. The purpose of going abroad to work was to have a better life, a better future. In fact, they would never stop, at least not until they had accumulated the fortune, they so coveted, not until they could go back home as wealthy men.

My grandfather gradually accustomed himself to life in Indonesia. Becoming a free man however, had not reduced his workload, quite the contrary. He worked for small rubber plantations, and paper factories, all businesses that had been established by coolies like him who had arrived a few years before him. Loneliness was working its way in him and was leading him to slowly forget about his hometown people and family. He began to actively participate in all sorts of local events and activities. In this way he developed a very close relationship with a local family, and in this family, there was young lady named Luo Mei. Luo Mei's beauty made my grandfather forget even about that girl from his old village, for whom he had longed for so long. He could tell that Luo Mei had good feelings about him too. So, although penniless, my bold Grandfather took on himself to ask Luo Mei's parents for her hand. He had not expected however, that Luo Mei's parents would so gladly and readily agree to his proposal.

Luo Mei was born in Indonesia, and she was the sixth and youngest daughter of the Luo Family. Luo Mei's parents had always hoped to have a son to perpetuate the family's lineage. Still, much to their dismay, their sixth child had turned out to be another girl, and at that point, they did not have the courage to keep trying their luck. All they wanted now was to marry off their daughters as soon as possible, in doing so, they would not only save on grocery expenses, but they could also exploit their newfound sons-in-law, to make them work for free on their small rubber farm.

My grandfather took root in Indonesia and started a new life for himself there. After the wedding, he founded his own family. He and Luo Mei kept welcoming new members in it. In total, they raised four sons and four daughters. By the time his last son was born, grandfather still hadn't returned to China. His parents occasionally received money and gifts from him, that's how they knew things were going well for their son overseas. It put their minds to rest to know that he was safe and sound. In such an age of turmoil, separations and deaths were a common occurrence. People would bid farewell to each other, knowing full well they would never see each other again, without even a shed of tear, as if it was their fate, as if it was a normal fate. Back then, survival superseded everything else.

4. Jesus and Guanyin

My mother once told me that she was already bound by a deed made with Guanyin, also called Avalokitesvara Bodhisattva, by which my mom is the goddess' adoptive daughter. For this reason, she couldn't simply, as I wanted, change her faith and become a Christian. She did tell me however that she believed in the existence of Jesus, for having already seen him. It was the end of 1998, and my mother had come to Canada to take care of me and my newborn son, she stayed with us for a year. One morning, my mother had a heart attack, and I took her to the hospital. On the same day, she underwent a stent procedure.

We didn't have to wait for more than two days, before the doctor determined that a bypass surgery was necessary. On the night before her heart bypass surgery, my mother was lying alone on her hospital bed, where she had terrible nightmares all night long. She dreamed of three Westerners who had sneaked on top of her hospital room's curtains. They were staring at her with their weird looks. My mother was in a double room, where two beds were separated by curtains. What my mother told me about these "foreigners" left me in a state of shock. Her description corresponded perfectly to the devils of the Christian faith. I had never told her anything about devils or their appearance, so she could not know that what she saw as "foreigners" were devils. She also said that these "people" while lying atop the curtains, peered around surreptitiously and were discussing what they were about to do. She was terrified. By chance, that same day during the afternoon, my friends from the local church had come to see her and teach her how to pray. She remembered a few words of prayer and shouted out a few times, "Jesus save me!" Immediately, those three "people" appeared stunned and confused and looked at each other for a while, then disappeared in a burst of smoke.

When my mother was sick, my friends from the church would often come to visit her, take care of her, and evangelize her. My mother eventually recovered from her illness and as soon as she felt better, returned to Hong Kong. There, she discreetly removed the

Guanyin Jade pendant that I had given her a few decades back and that she had always kept wearing. She carefully placed it in the closet and never wore it again in her lifetime. However, she did not wear either the diamond cross pendant that I had also bought for her after immigrating to Canada. She didn't want to violate the deed that her father had sealed for her with Guanyin, but she couldn't forget either the protection that Jesus had once provided her.

The story of the birth of my mother is a story re-told time and again by my mother's father. It became a sort of legend known to all around him.

That day, my grandfather had gone out to sea to fish, but had departed two hours earlier than his usual time. My grandfather though was not a fisherman. He would usually rent a fishing boat to go out fishing for a short time. At that time, my grandfather and my grandmother Luo Mei had already had three sons and three daughters. The fresh fish that the whole family would eat that year depended entirely on the catches made during the two fishing trips that my grandfather would undertake during that year. At that time, Luo Mei was often anxious and restless, her temper was getting increasingly difficult. My grandfather hoped he could take advantage of this time out to sea to make a bigger catch. That way he could sell the surplus and make some money to buy a gift for Luo Mei, and hopefully brighten her mood a little.

Grandfather was toiling hard on his boat, throwing away and pulling back his net, but regardless of his efforts, the harvest was pitiful. A few small yellow croaker fish and some tiny shrimps, these could serve in his own kitchen, but a trip to the fish market to sell them off would not be worthwhile.

The sun was about to set behind the mountains and my grandfather was listlessly scouring the horizon over the boundless sea. He felt sour and all he could see was the sun's golden glitter over the sea's surface and the dazzling reflection of that light brought on by the waves. A city suddenly faintly appeared in the distance, and by looking at it, my grandfather could even catch a glimpse of the people walking there on the street, far away. The scene strongly reminded my grandfather of his hometown, to the extent that he wondered if he had inadvertently drifted back home. "I can't possibly be back home !?" For a moment my grandfather was so startled, he lost his balance, his feet slipped, and he fell into the sea. By chance, he was an experienced swimmer and he quickly made it back onto the boat. Once back on board however, when he looked back again toward that city, it was nowhere to be seen. But even though it had disappeared from the horizon, his hometown was still very much present in his mind, and he felt a great sadness swell up in him, for he had left it for so many years, and for he hadn't even ever gone back to visit his parents. He could not restrain the tremendous shame and remorsefulness he felt and burst into tears.

Sitting alone in the middle of a soundless sea, Grandfather did not know for how long he had been crying there. The sea was now pitch-black, and Grandfather was finally "awakening" from his emotional outburst. He decided to throw the net for one last time. Regardless of how much he could catch this time, he would head back home after. He had to return the boat and Luo Mei and the children were quite certainly all waiting for him at home. Just as Grandfather was dragging the fishing net back onto the boat and preparing to throw it back into the sea, he saw a person standing at the bow of his ship.

That person was dressed in a long white gown and stood there, facing him. Because of the brightness of that person's clothing, Grandfather couldn't see precisely what the person looked like. He could see however a few long ribbons of that bright gown fluttering in the sea wind. What was even stranger however, was that my grandfather, facing this stranger standing on his boat, was not even scared and quite the contrary, he felt warmth and peacefulness. When that person finally spoke to him, Grandfather did not hear his voice through his ears: the words seemed to be conveyed directly into his mind. “Yang Yong, do not be afraid, do not miss the people of your hometown any longer. Concentrate on building your life here, and you will have my protection. I bring you gifts today.” The person then lifted a white vase it held in its hand and poured from it a few drops of water into the sea, while reciting in a low voice what appeared to be prayers. In its other hand, the person was holding a little baby, and at that moment, the person gently approached Yang Yong to show the baby to him. After a short while, it took the baby back. As Grandfather saw the little baby looking toward him and smiling, he simply knew not what to do, and as if in a dream, the person holding the baby slowly drifted up toward the sky and flew toward this dark sea’s bright moon.

5. Mooney

Yang Yong would never forget the moon of that night, its exceptional brightness and not only would he not forget, but he would also tell everyone whom he knew about the supernatural events he went through that night. He would on every occasion, add details and enhance his story. He was convinced that the "person" who was standing at the bow of his boat was Guanyin, the Buddhist Goddess. How Guanyin appeared to him, what Guanyin promised him, and how much fish he caught with his last throw of net after meeting the Goddess, these descriptions in his story were always becoming more colorful and incredible with each telling.

That last net that Yang Yong threw that night, when he dragged it back from the sea, it was indeed full of large, rare and valuable fish, the kind that's not easy to catch. Grandfather returned home with his prize and the next day early in the morning, he sold his fish on the market. As per his word, the money he got from selling the fish was not only enough for him to expand and renovate his small shabby cottage, but it was also enough for him to go back to China to visit his family. However, the details of this long-awaited trip, and what happened to Yang Yong while he was gone, remain a mystery to this day. There is in fact not a soul who knows anything about it, Yang Yong kept it that way.

After returning from his Chinese hometown, Yang Yong no longer climbed up that big tree where he used to set his gaze toward the north. The curved and sinuous lakes that fascinated him so much had lost all their appeal. His mind was now firmly set on staying in Indonesia.

In 1923, my grandfather returned from China. Not long after his return Luo Mei gave birth to their fourth daughter, my mother. My Grandfather named my mother "Yue Niang", meaning girl from the moon, so we will call her "Mooney" in this book. Mooney was light-skinned with a fair complexion; she did not look like she was the child of a rustic agrarian family. Yang Yong believed that Mooney was in fact the baby that Guanyin was holding in its arms on that mystic night at sea. When Mooney reached her first month of age, he took her to the Guanyin Temple, and there he sealed the deed with Guanyin, whereas his daughter Mooney was to be dedicated to the Goddess. On the same occasion, he decided that all his family should convert to the cult of Guanyin, and consequently, from now on, the consumption of beef was prohibited in his household.

Mooney was as bright as she was beautiful, she had a kind of indescribable inner calm. Additionally, she was the adoptive daughter of Guanyin. My grandfather doted particularly on his little Mooney. He was not willing to let her work the field like the others; he would only set her onto more feminine tasks like sewing. Even after having matured in age, her only task was still just to make clothes for the family of ten. Two years after the birth of Mooney, the Yang family once more welcomed a baby boy. Time went by neither too quickly nor too slowly as Yang Yong worked hard to raise his four sons and four daughters. As his three elder boys grew up, they began to work as helpers in a Dutch tobacco plantation, the family gradually increased its income through their labor and its circumstances kept improving.

Mooney had a skilled hand and at a time when there were no sewing machines, she could produce a garment all by herself, from choosing the fabrics, to the tailoring, she could do it all stitch by stitch with just a needle. Due to my mother's great craftsmanship, her family became the most well-dressed and decent looking in the small village they inhabited. Occasionally, when there was a birthday or a wedding or some other event in the village, other families would come to my grandfather's doorstep to ask him, or rather beg him, to let his little girl from the moon "Mooney" sew new clothes for them to attend the event.

Grandfather was a great talker, skilled at the art of speech, and his house was very much frequented by his friends, who often crowded-out the place. He welcomed even some strangers who, due to his reputation, were coming sometimes to listen to him. Luo Mei was a very diligent and capable woman. When the women of the nearby families had difficulties of any sort, the first person they would think of was her. They would come to consult her and ask her to come up with ideas for their issues. The Yang family with four sons and four daughters was a prosperous one. Among them, the third son was fascinated by the legends told by his father about the miracles performed by ancient doctors in traditional Chinese medicine, and based on these legends, he began going to the mountains to find medicinal herbs and to learn medicine all by himself. Whenever a family member had a fever, a dizziness, or a stomachache, he would prepare and decoct his herbal medicine for them, and surprisingly, the patients would all recover. His success encouraged him, and he became more confident in his abilities. Using the story of his father's encounter with the goddess Guanyin, He began to treat patients from both the village and from outside the village using his own medicine. He used to tell his patients that the secret herbal recipes had been handed down to his family, through his father, from the goddess herself. Fortunately, the patients who came to see him were all consulting for minor illnesses, so he was able to cure them easily. Gradually, the Yang family became "famous" all around.

All the children soon reached the age of founding their own families, the three older sons made-do with what was in their surroundings and married local girls from nearby households. Although Yang Yong and Luo Mei had married out of their own wills, when the time came for their daughters to marry, my grandfather decided to stick to the old Chinese custom, whereby without the "benediction from the parents, and introduction by a matchmaker", there would be no marriage.

6. Words of the Matchmaker

Whenever my mother would tell me that the first time she and my father met was on the night of their wedding, it made me laugh, and to think that this was a common fact of life just half a century ago illustrates just how fast the world changes. How many such old things had the people of my generation seen fade out? and the introduction of how many new things had they witnessed? Back in 1994, I can still clearly remember, I had already moved to Canada, and I was working in a large company. The company I was in was trying to modernize and the old office employees strongly opposed the proposed changes to the means of communication, the company wanted to replace the fax machines for e-mails. Ten years later, is there still anyone on the office-job market unable to use a computer? In 2017, is there anyone not using social media on a regular basis? “Benediction from the parents, and introduction by a matchmaker” has become a joke. Would any young adult today in China still live by such customs, follow such rituals?

But let’s get back to our main topic, the marriage of my mother to my father. It was a deed entirely arranged, single-handedly managed by my grandfather, and looking at it today, I feel like there was really nothing wrong about this “arranged marriage”. Although my parents didn’t get to grow old together, when I think about their marriage and I compare it to those of other couples that formed out of free will, well they too had quarrels, misunderstandings and reconciliations, but in the end, I believe that my parent ‘s marriage was at least ten times better.

When Yang Yong “went foreign” and left China for Indonesia, he was young and rebellious, however as he grew older, his character changed, and he became increasingly conservative and old-fashioned. In his opinion, the ancestor’s old rules and lessons had prevalence over everything else, and they had to be followed. He relied entirely on the old-fashioned way of thinking on the matter of choosing husbands for his daughters. He would not allow his daughters to find love freely. His own marriage was a free choice, and this may have been another reason why he wanted to manage his daughter's marriage. He and Luo Mei had been quarreling for decades, and it had left a sense of frustration in him. He imagined that if there had been a matchmaker handling matters for him, maybe he could have had a better match, a wife better suited to him.

To choose husbands for his three older daughters, he followed the same procedure.

The first step was to find a local matchmaker who had a good reputation, Yang would then give her a briefing about his daughter, and then ask her to select young men, giving her a list of criteria of what he was looking for in a son-in-law. On receiving the "command" of Yang Yong, the matchmaker would diffuse the news everywhere and she would personally visit some men of the appropriate age. She would then report back to Yang Yong, giving him information on the single men interested in marrying into the Yang family. There were more young women than young men in Indonesia at that time, so finding a suitable man was easier said than done.

In the second step, a selection is made of the several men who seem to be a good match for his daughter. Yang Yong would then arrange for these men to come to the house as guests. Of course, they wouldn't come all at once. These appointments are private and made on an individual basis. During the meeting, Yang Yong would seek to clarify the details surrounding the man's background, including the circumstances of his birth, his character and his general abilities. Yang Yong was not looking for a man of great fortune. Back then, even if a man owned a gold mine, all it took was for a war to break out, and he could then very quickly lose everything. "A lotus leaf can be filled with pearly dew, but none of it will survive a gust of wind." When choosing a son-in-law, Yang Yong especially valued the man's ability to support a family. The man had to have a viable trade, skills to make a living, and resilience was key.

During that meeting, the daughter to be married was still not involved whatsoever. This was a negotiation between two men. Involving everyone at that stage would feel awkward, and the man would simply, likely, politely take his leave. This meeting was, for all intent and purpose, just a polite visit by a yet-not-so familiar young man. However, if both men had a good feeling about each other, Yang Yong would then give a shout toward the back of the living room. His wife Luo Mei knew in advance that this was a secret code, a signal from her husband. She would then task her to-be-married daughter to bring a plate of tea and pastries to the guest for his enjoyment. At that moment, still completely unbeknownst to the daughter, the guest in the living room would take a good look at her, and if he found himself satisfied, he would become her husband, the person she would spend the rest of her life with.

The third step was to negotiate the betrothal gifts. Though Yang Yong was not selling his daughter, the money was an indispensable part of the deed. The parents of the bride considered the gifts a representation of the young man's sincerity toward his bride. What Yang Yong was asking for "gifts", was that in addition to the expenses of the wedding, that the man paid him the entirety of his income for the first two years of labor after the marriage. And Yang Yong would take charge of managing the daily expenses of the newly weds during that time.

Over the course of a few years, Yang Yong consecutively successfully married off his three older daughters. Regardless of his multiple apprehensions about the matter, it would eventually be Mooney's turn. Mooney was almost 19 years old, and that was older than the age of all her sisters when they were married. Yang Yong was determined to find an outstanding young man for his beloved Mooney, one that was even better that those he had found for his other daughters.

7. The Young Wen Quan

Yang Yong was preparing the request he intended to give the matchmaker for the recruitment of his new son-in-law. He wanted to find a husband of a different kind for his little daughter Mooney.

Coincidentally, this afternoon, Yang Yong's neighbor Uncle Oyster came over to discuss with him. He told him there was a young man who had come back from China bringing local products and specialties for the ancients of their region. To make things easier for the guest who had travelled a great deal, Uncle Oyster said, "Why not ask him to come directly to your home." We could invite everyone to come have tea at the same time, and it would allow more time for the guest to talk about his journey to China, to bring us up to date on our hometown. Yang Yong agreed to the request of Uncle Oyster without giving it much thought, as he did not expect this meeting to be of any particular importance.

That evening, Uncle Oyster led a young man of average height to Yang Yong's home, he looked young, but very mature for his age. He was wearing a well-fitting western-style suit and looked quite different from the other boys who came from the country. He had used a shiny hair wax to neatly slick back his hair, and he looked quite the businessman.

The young man, all-smiling, stepped into Yang's house with confidence and went straight to Yang Yong to shake hands with him. He stated his name loud and clear: "My name is Liu Wen Quan, and I just made the trip from Haifeng to 'Solo' (an Indonesian city with a large population of Chinese immigrants). I came specially to visit all the folks from our village." The young man then shook hands with everyone in the room. The young man's grasp had left an impression on Yang Yong.

Liu Wen Quan was like a spring breeze from these old men's hometown. His speech, his demeanor and his insight formed an aura around him. It didn't take long for him to seduce the ten or so guests who were present in Yang Yong's home that day.

Yang Yong put on his new glasses, and carefully "inspected" the young man in front of him. He then couldn't help but begin to tell him about what he experienced when he returned home about twenty years ago. He had never told anyone else about it. Yang Yong said that the year he returned to China, he found chaos in his hometown, there were constant natural disasters, and pirates were rampant. Yang Yong felt scared and desperate. Part of him just wanted to run away, but he just felt too ashamed to do so, he felt that he would be betraying the descendants of the Yang family who had been so loyal in defending the country during the Northern Song Dynasty. He struggled internally for a long time, not knowing what to do. In the end, he couldn't sacrifice himself for his country, so he chose to return to his life in Indonesia. He decided to never return to China again and resolved to stay in this foreign country and take root.

"Our roots however are still where our ancestors lived for generations. Our departure is but temporary. In a not-so-distant future, we will all return to our source, return to our hometown. We have our loved ones there and the land we love." After listening to Yang Yong, Liu Wen Quan, impassioned, responded enthusiastically. He expressed his understanding of Yang Yong's decision back then. He said that there had been great change in his hometown during the past ten years. He started his speech by talking about the peasant association founded by the agrarian movement leader from his hometown Haifeng, Peng Pai.

Then he talked about how the farmers in his hometown resisted and fought the landlords. Although Peng Pai was assassinated in the end, the revolutionary spark he ignited did not vanish. Young Wen Quan believed that the seed of revolution planted by his predecessors would inevitably grow, burning down the old society, and then surely giving rise to the new society.

"When that happens, our sons will not have to be sold as coolies like us anymore. They won't have to travel across the ocean to go to someone else's country and beg for a living, to always depend on someone else's goodwill and be a de-facto third-class citizen." Liu Wen Quan's words resonated in the room. He depicted an ideal country, and everyone in the room was moved. That day, Liu Wen Quan left a lasting and very positive impression on Yang Yong.

When he woke up the next morning, Yang Yong rushed to see Uncle Oyster, and asked for more details about the background of Liu Wen Quan. He learned that Liu's father was also a coolie in Indonesia when he was young, but unlike him, after fulfilling his contract, he did not stay but returned to his hometown instead. He eventually moved to Haifeng, where he depended on the good financial situation of some of his relatives for a while before he eventually married and had children in Shanwei. Wen Quan was the oldest child of the Liu family. When Liu Wen Quan turned sixteen, Liu's father decided to bring his wife and Wen Quan, as well as Wen Quan's younger brother, and his sister back to Indonesia. Once back there, the Liu family had another son. At the age of seventeen, Liu Wen Quan had begun taking on the responsibility of supporting a family. In a small town mainly inhabited by Chinese, he and his father opened a grocery store that specialized in selling incense sticks. The whole family of six depended on this small shop for their living.

"Is Liu Wen Quan married?" Yang Yong couldn't resist immediately asking. Uncle Oyster visibly bothered, replied that to the best of his knowledge, Quan was single. Yang Yong then asked Uncle Oyster to arrange for Liu Wen Quan to visit him again, saying he would prepare a salty tea, a delicacy in their hometown.

8. The Marriage

"Have you ever thought of getting married?" The third serving of tea hadn't yet been poured before Yang Yong went straight to the subject.

"I have thought about it, but I haven't met the right person yet." Liu Wen Quan replied.

"I have a little daughter called Mooney. She's beautiful, skillful and smart." Yang Yong went straight to it.

"Should I call her out, so you can have a look at her?" Seeing Liu Wen Quan was embarrassed to answer, Yang Yong lost no time and barked loudly toward the inner house.

"Zhang, bring some more hot tea for the guest, and bring some pastries as well."

"Zhang" was the nickname of my mother Mooney, "Zhang" meant "long plaits" in South Fujian dialect. When my mother was a child, she wore two long black plaits, they were beautiful, so everyone called her "Zhang".

"Zhang" heard her father calling, and hurriedly cut out pieces from the tray of tapioca cake that had just been steamed in the morning and placed them on a small porcelain plate. She poured hot water into a teapot, where tea leaves had already been placed and holding the plate of pastries with one hand, and carrying the teapot with the other, she ran out to the living room. The pastries and tea pot were both very hot, so after placing them on the table, she quickly took to rubbing her two small hands together and put them close to her mouth to try to blow away the heat while jumping uncontrollably on her feet out of pain.

Liu Wen Quan, taken by the scene, found the girl's manners quite adorable. He took the occasion to quietly gaze at her. He noticed she was wearing an ample water-blue skirt that covered beyond the knee. The garment was embroidered with an image of a child riding a bicycle on a flowery meadow. The girl had delicate features, she was calm and composed and he was moved. Mooney felt someone staring at her, so she looked up at him, and their eyes met. She instinctively responded with a nervous smile and quickly left the room. Liu Wen Quan, off-balance, had a “strange feeling”, his face was still red from the blushing he had when she smiled at him.

Yang Yong seeing how these two children looked at each other, inwardly rejoiced. He was especially reinforced in his view that these two were a match by Mooney’s smile toward Wen Quan. Mooney was usually proud and slightly haughty, she wouldn’t engage conversations with strangers, and even less smile at them. Her gentle smile at Quan that day looked like a sign of fate.

Liu Wen Quan had fallen in love with Mooney at first sight. On that same day, as per Yang Yong’s wishes, Quan officially asked Yang Yong for Mooney’s hand. Yang Yong readily agreed to the proposal. Since Yang had a very high opinion of Liu, and because he didn’t see him as “just another fish in the bowl”, He rescinded his rule “the son-in-law has to work for the father-in-law for two years.” Mooney was an obedient daughter. She did not know with whom her father might want her to marry, but she trusted her father and his decisions. So come the wedding night, she believed that she was seeing her husband for the first time. She had no recollection of their first meeting at her father's house. It is only after the wedding, when Quan made a joke about the first time, they met each other in Yang's living room, that Mooney remembered that fateful evening.

Mooney and Quan's love story really began after the marriage.

After the marriage, Mooney moved to live with Wen Quan's family. Compared to her days as a daughter in her father's house, she had it much harder. She had to cook for the entire Liu family every day, and she had to take care of the two younger brothers, and a younger sister of her husband. The oldest of the two brothers of Wen Quan was 19 years old, the sister was 16 years old, and the youngest brother was eight years old. Mooney's new parents-in-law treated her relatively gently, her new mother-in-law however did not have much drive for doing her house chores. Mooney's arrival in her house was a relief to her, as she seized the opportunity and delegated all of her tasks and responsibilities to the newly-weds.

Fortunately, the young couple at least was deeply in love. They were of the same mind and combined their efforts toward their goals. Their family was a blooming garden, and Liu Wen Quan's businesses were booming. In addition to the grocery store, he had also started some other businesses with friends. Wen Quan cherished Mooney endlessly, so he hired two Indonesian maids to help her with her house chores. After getting this help, Mooney finally had some spare time, which she used in part to make some new clothes for the family. Quan's brother regularly wore suits made by his new sister-in-law. He used to stroll around, showing off to everyone in his fine attire, and did not fail to attract many young girls' attention.

In 1945, Liu Wen Quan and Mooney's first child was born. One month later that same year, Mooney's mother-in-law also gave birth to their youngest daughter.

9. Husband and Children

It is said among the people that a woman who gives birth to three sons and two daughters will be rich and prosperous for the rest of her life.

Fortunately, enough, my mother gave birth to three sons and two daughters. And indeed, she did enjoy the luxuries of life for a while, but in these turbulent times, the fate of the people could not withstand that of the country. After her forties had passed, my mother began to drift about the continent. She used to say that she was like a snail, traveling with her house on her back, and that wherever she went, that place was home. She suffered through many hardships, and in the end, she didn't get to grow old rich and prosperous, in her last days I don't even think she owned her own bed.

The year I was born, my father's businesses were repeatedly being robbed and torched by Indonesians, and the family's fortune was in decline. My brothers and sister nostalgically remembered the times when they lived in villas in Medan, when they had servants and drivers, these are all things I could never enjoy. In my childhood memories, to scrape a living my mother had to work endless hours sewing clothes for customers. I remember that when we were in Macau, we once almost ran out of food completely. My poor mother then asked me to deliver the clothes she had just finished sewing for a customer, and upon delivery I received fifteen Macau dollars from said customer. As soon as I got home my mother took me to the market to buy all she could afford with that paltry sum, five pounds of rice, and half a catty of oil.

In Hong Kong, land is worth ten times more than gold. So back then, when we were living there, I could not afford to provide my ageing mother with a cozy hearth and lavish lifestyle. And today my mother has passed away, so even if I could, I can't give her back now all that she's given me. This is by far my life's greatest regret.

In the winter of 1969, Mooney took her youngest daughter Xilian with her, and bid farewell to her husband, Liu Wen Quan. She left Indonesia, never to return. The plane took off from the capital of Indonesia, Jakarta. In my mother's heart, there was a balance, and it had begun to tilt. On one side, there was her husband, and on the other, her three sons and daughter. One side clearly weighed more than the other.

The plane landed at Hong Kong's Kai Tak Airport at dusk. Xilian didn't feel like she was just sitting on a plane, in her child's mind she saw herself as a small flying bird, freely flitting about in the sky. She flew down from the sky and flanked by a dense forest of buildings on both sides, traversed the city. The plane landed on a magnificently lighted tarmac. The little Xilian had never seen such a beautiful lighting before. On the day they left Indonesia, her mother told her that they were going to a beautiful place, where she could go to a "real" school. In fact, from the age of two, Xilian began to "go to school", but she never really went to a real school because at that time in Indonesia, the government had implemented anti-Chinese policies, and all Chinese schools had been forced to close. The Chinese people could not learn Chinese in schools, so my father found a private teacher for her young daughter. A female teacher came to the house every day and gave classes to Xilian, tutoring her in Chinese and mathematics. My father also secretly subscribed to magazines from Hong Kong such as "Children's Paradise". Being able to go to a real school with other children had been Xilian's greatest desire since her youngest age.

The agents at the Hong Kong customs knew the destination of the mother and daughter was Macau, so they granted them both a visa for a stay of no more than a week. It hadn't been necessary however as Mooney and her daughter did not stay in Hong Kong for more than a day. They had arranged for people to pick them up at the airport and take them directly to the Hong Kong-Macau Ferry terminal at the Shun Tak Centre in Sheung Wan. After sunset, they were ferried to Macau.

This was my first journey. From this day on, as if cursed by a naughty little demon, I've had to keep travelling between different countries and regions. Even today, I am still travelling non-stop, from North America to Asia, with stays in Europe. I can't remember if I was carrying a luggage on my first trip, but I do remember that my mother, holding my little hand, was walking me from customs to customs.

I remember as well that day's bleak weather. I was wearing a light-yellow fluffy coat that my mother had sewed for me. Underneath, I wore a light-pink dress over a pair of white socks. I also had a pair of small leather black shoes. My whole outfit was brand-new, I felt as if I was headed for a banquet. I wasn't sad at all about leaving Indonesia, so during the whole trip my excitation hadn't wavered.

My mother however was visibly and relentlessly worried. At the age of Forty-three, accompanied by her little girl, she was moving to an unfamiliar new land, where the people and the customs were both unknown, where even the language presented a challenge of its own. And on top of that, she had to carry out a crucial mission. Her goal on this journey was to bring back to her side her four children who had returned to China a few years ago to "study", and regardless of the hardships she would have to face in doing so, she was resolved to not let her children remain in this "dangerous" land.

10. Returning to China

Xilian had only some fragments of memory about her days in Indonesia. Some of her memories could have been influenced by her young imagination, some others might have been pure fiction. She was so unsure, she didn't dare assume any of these memories were genuine, she couldn't tell what had happened from what she may have imagined. It is only much later, as she was actively searching through the past to find out what had happened, that the real facts emerged from these originally vague old memories.

Among Xilian's fuzzy memories, there was one where she remembered her father coming back home after a trip of a few days looking terrified. She remembers him saying to her mother: "The killings began outside, the police are carrying away carts full of bodies." My mother was petrified. My father tried to comfort her, saying he would find a way. Xilian had never heard anything about people getting killed before, so that scene remained engraved in her memory.

As Xilian grew up, no one around her had ever mentioned this massacre. Anti-Chinese measures were often implemented in Indonesia and the Chinese who had left Indonesia preferred to forget about it. No one wanted to delve back into these sad stories. In 2012, the documentary "The act of killing" was nominated for an Oscar, the events of the 30th of September 1965 in Indonesia were clearly exposed to the public for the first time. Xilian then realized how terrifying and dangerous it had been for her and her family to live there back then, they could have been killed at any time.

The four brothers and sister of Xilian were being sent back to mainland China as they reached the age of twelve to thirteen years old. Xilian's eldest brother returned to China in 1959. Accompanying him was his grandmother, his uncles and aunts, as well as his parents who had received an invitation to participate in the grand ceremony of the 10th anniversary of the founding of the New China. During the journey, it was arranged for the patriotic overseas Chinese to visit a great number of attractions and everywhere they went, they were met with the sight of a prosperous people living in utopia, it was thrilling and breath-taking and it would leave people with a sense of excitement. Wen Quan could not suppress the enthusiasm he felt, and all trip long he kept thinking about how he could participate in the construction of this New China. He hated that he couldn't immediately drop everything else to serve his motherland.

Xilian's paternal grandfather died at a young age and her paternal grandmother stayed with her son in Indonesia. Xilian's father, Liu Wen Quan, was a capable and smart person. The family of more than ten's entire livelihood depended on him. As time went by, his businesses kept growing and aside from the grocery store, he ran a paper mill, and a rubber plantation. He also worked as a director in some Chinese community associations.

His household employed several helpers and among them, there was a tall and handsome man from Shandong. He was about the age of Wen Quan's mother and whenever they had free time, he and she would often get together to chat and exchange pleasantries. Not long after however the man resigned his position and returned to China. Xilian's grandmother was dispirited by his departure, and she eventually got depressed. She was brooding all day, and she even hid in places to weep in silence. Wen Quan could not bear seeing his mother in such a state so he asked her what could make her feel better. His mother answered that she too, wanted to return to China.

In September of 1959, a cruise ship named "Zhi Li hua" carried Liu Wen Quan's mother, Liu Wen Quan's two younger brothers and two younger sisters, as well as his own eldest son Zhi Wen back to China. They carried with them fifteen Singer brand sewing machines, hundreds of rolls of various fabrics, all kinds of food, dozens of boxes of different products, a broad array of merchandise, impressive both in volume and variety. They were setting sail for China as a rich and glamorous family.

On their arrival, Liu Wen Quan allocated a vast sum to build a large new house for the family there. The house had a place for a shop on the ground floor, there were eight large rooms and a backyard garden, where a small well had been dug to supply drinking water for the family. This "overseas Chinese house" was the envy of the neighborhood. Quan's plan was to have his youngest brother and eldest son attend university there, to have his other younger brother open a garment factory, and to make sure his two younger sisters would be around to accompany their mother in her old age.

In 1960, Liu Wen Quan's second son, Zhi Wu, embarked on that same cruise ship to return to China. He brought alongside him seven wooden boxes, which occupied about half the size of a shipping container, fourteen large luggage, ten expensive Swiss watches, and an oil barrel filled with baby powder. Hidden in the barrel's content was a bag of diamonds that Quan intended to donate to the Chinese government.

In 1966, Liu Wen Quan sent his third son Zhi Qiang and his daughter, Xi Zhi, back to China. For this trip however the children did not board the cruise boat, they took a plane that departed from the Indonesian capital Jakarta instead. Along with them were the children of good friends of Liu Wen Quan, they were a total of eleven persons making the trip back to China together.

Once back in China, Xilian's two elder brothers finished their secondary school, and after passing admission exams, were fortunate enough to be admitted into a university. The third brother and sister however did not even have a chance to reach secondary school, they first had to complete a year at the Fujian Overseas Chinese Tutoring School, to attain educational standards, and then the ten years long Chinese Cultural Revolution began. All the young people who had returned to China from overseas were assigned to rural villages to "learn from the peasants". My brother and sister were sent to the rural Tian Men County of the Hubei Province.

During the 1960s, the Great Chinese mainland experienced a succession of both natural and man-made disasters. The sewing machines that Liu Wen Quan had brought to China with the intention of opening a garment factory, were all liquidated piece-by-piece by his younger brother. In a time marked by famine and misery, his newly married young brother could afford to proudly walk the streets wearing shining leather shoes and regularly took family members to lavish restaurants.

Among those who returned to China with the third brother and the sister of Xilian, there was one boy who was killed by a young man of an opposite faction during a "fight" that took place during the ten years long ('66-'76) Chinese Cultural Revolution. The boy killed was his family's only child and in order to not let his parents suffer the blow such a news would bring them, the irresponsible and immature children that accompanied him took turns writing letters to his parents, impersonating him, to report that he was safe and sound. When Mooney learned about this incident, she decided to move to Macau immediately.

The paternal grandmother of Xilian was never able to meet again with the Shandong man she had grown so fond of.

11. Leaving China

Seven-year-old Xilian moved to Macau with her mother.

They initially lived in a small room they rented from a friend's friend. Mooney then found a primary school for Xilian, but because the little girl had never studied in a school before, she had to pass exams that would determine her level. She did very well in the tests and was directly placed in fourth grade. In her classroom she felt much like an alien at first however, as she didn't yet speak the language. Fortunately for them, the people of Macau were simple and down-to-earth with a generous and good heart. Everyone was willing to help them. Xilian quickly learned the local language, Cantonese, and eventually got along very well with her classmates.

As soon as Xilian was settled in school, Mooney could begin her mission of actively applying for her children to leave mainland China. Among her four children, the eldest son studied agriculture, and after graduating from university, he was dispatched to Hainan Island. There he got married and had a baby girl. The second son studied Geology. After graduation, he was directly sent to do exploration work in the country's forested and mountainous regions. The younger son and the daughter couldn't finish their middle school. The revolution had begun, and they were sent on farms, under the Chinese government's slogan "to learn from the peasants". They worked as farmers there for years, their wage was not sufficient to pay for their own food, so along the years they accumulated a debt toward the Commune.

Mooney's priority was to head for Wuhan. Her thinking was to go first for her two younger children who were about 20 years old. She wanted to arrange a new life for them as soon as possible. She would take a long-distance bus from Macau to Guangzhou, then a train from Guangzhou to Wuhan. Once in Wuhan, she still had to endure ten hours of jolting in a bus before reaching her children's countryside location.

Once installed in the village's guest house, she would begin to report herself to the police station every day, she met the head of the Public Security Bureau on several occasions, to beg him to approve her application for her children to leave China. She sometimes brought Xilian with her, the two would quietly sit for hours in the police station hoping for news. Most of the time however, to avoid hindering the child's academic progress, she left Xilian in Macau.

She would pay some friends to take care of her, and little Xilian who was staying with these family's unknown to her, behaved cautiously and politely, she didn't dare speak out loud, or make noise of any sort.

Xilian's eldest brother and his wife however were quite worried about the applications made by Xilian's mother for them to leave China. They figured it could have a negative impact on their life going forward. They wrote a letter to the Public Security Bureau, to indicate that the mother's actions were hers only, that her intention for them to leave China was not shared by them and that she had not obtained their consent prior to making these applications. They wrote that they both had no intention of leaving the country, and the applications in their name were cancelled by the Bureau.

From 1972 to 1973, after countless trials and tribulations, after making the trip back and forth from Macau to to mainland China countless times, Mooney finally succeeded in bringing back three of her children, the eldest one having stayed, and she helped bring back as well the children of other relatives and friends, for a total of eight persons. Upon leaving China, the children could obtain a one-way pass to either Macau or Hong Kong, the choice was up to them.

At that time, Macau belonged to the Portuguese government and Hong Kong belonged to the British Empire. Macau's Portuguese government had always cooperated with the Chinese government, and they were willing to accept new immigrants unconditionally. Hong Kong's British government however would balk at accepting immigrants who were born in Indonesia, they didn't want to add onto themselves the burden of taking them in, so they generally tried to send them back to Indonesia. To avoid unnecessary complications, most Indonesian-born Chinese who wanted to leave for Hong-Kong changed their birthplace to China.

Mooney applied for her youngest son and daughter to move to Macau, as she hoped to keep them by her side. The second son went to Hong Kong. The eldest son eventually agreed to apply to leave China and was able to move to Hong Kong with his family two years later.

Mooney's younger son and daughter had been played by fate. Just as they had returned to China, the Cultural Revolution had begun. Their opportunity to attend school and gain an education was denied. When they made their way back to Macau, they had reached their 20's and were too old to start high school. Their best option was to serve as unskilled labor in garment factories.

Upon leaving China, the eldest son with his wife and daughter were assigned by the Hong Kong government to the Kowloon Bay camp. This resettlement area was made-up of rows of simple and rudimentary aluminum-sheet plated houses, each house was about ten square meters, in each of them there was a bed and some simple furniture. They had to cook on their door sill outside the house and there were public toilets at the end of each row of houses. This kind of resettlement area was used by the government to lodge new immigrants, as well as refugees, generally the people who lived in the mountains, and whose houses had been demolished to make room for building new high-rise apartments.

The living conditions in the resettlement area were poor, especially during the summer, the oven-like heat was nearly unbearable. Against all expectations however, the resettlement area was relatively safe. The newcomers had a roof over their heads at least and although life was difficult, everyone had hope for a better future. A few years later, the Hong Kong government demolished the resettlement area. All the camp's families were moved to a public housing building, where the living conditions were much better.

The introverted second son lived alone in a rented room after graduating. He kept studying while working daytime, to add to his academic curriculum. He was eager to move to Hong-Kong, as he longed to blend into that city's lifestyle. As it is said, Heaven does not let down the deserving. He gradually made his way up in the French company he worked for, married and had a baby girl. He and his wife saved a lot by leading a lifestyle marked by thrift and frugality. They then bought an apartment in the lofty area of Hong Kong Island and actively invested in the stock market. They were able to retire before turning 50 and emigrated to Canada to enjoy their golden age.

12. Macau and Hong Kong

Mooney and Wen Quan's five children were named in order: "Wen (art) Wu (Valiant) Qiang (Strength) Zhi (Ganoderma) and Lian (Lotus)". Within the Liu family genealogy, the boys were all named as per a forty words long poem, which showed the "Acts of living". As per this poem, this generation of sons had to be named using the middle name "Zhi" (Ambition). The daughters however did not have to be named as per the poem. The tradition in the southern Chinese province of Canton was for the girls to marry men of a different family name, and then take their husband's name. After the marriage they retained no association with their original family. Once married the daughters couldn't inherit from their original family's estate, and neither were they allowed to participate in the Qing Ming festival, where their former family honored their ancestors, they could not obtain that blessing.

Liu Wen Quan did not want to give up on his Indonesian businesses, so Mooney took Zhiqiang, Xizhi, and Xilian to live with her in Macau. The children grew up and their original residence became too small for them all. As Mooney was thinking about moving to a larger property, one night, she dreamed of a villa with a garden. The next day at dawn, she went to consult a real estate agent. As their first visit, the agent took her to a house on the gorgeous Bishop Street. There was a small tree in front of the house and that tree was the same as in her dream of the last night. She was thrilled and decided to rent the house immediately, despite the high rent, which she, likely, could not afford.

When she moved into this four-large-bedrooms house, Mooney simply painted two of the rooms and rented them out to four international students from Indonesia who were studying in Macau. This large house was expensive and the income from the accommodation of these four students was far from enough.

From time to time, Wen Quan would send out money to his wife from Indonesia. However, because of Indonesia's capital controls, he had to transfer the money via underground channels. Before sending the funds, he'd write a letter to his wife using a secret code. The seven characters "Zhong Hua Ren Min Gong He Guo "(which stood for People's Republic of China) represented 1, 2, 3, 4, 5, 6 and 7, respectively. The names of his five children stood for quantities "Wen" for one, "Wu" for ten, "Qiang" for hundred, "Zhi" for thousand and "Lian" for ten thousand. For example, if he wrote "Gong Zhi" is coming, please pick her up, it meant that he would send out five thousand Hong Kong dollars on a certain day of the month, specified in the letter. As anti-Chinese activities were still frequent in Indonesia, Quan's businesses had become just a shadow of their former selves. Shops were often burned down or pillaged, and he was cheated and blackmailed for money. Wen Quan's financial situation wasn't what it once was, and it wasn't improving. The frequency of his remittances to his family were always decreasing, and the code word "Lian" never even appeared in any of his letters to his wife.

The owner of the villa rented by Mooney was a mysterious woman of about sixty years old who always came by unaccompanied. From her clothes and appearance, it was impossible to tell that she was such a rich woman. As Mooney later discovered, she was the owner of several houses on Bishop Street. Two years after Mooney rented the house, she suddenly announced to all her tenants that she was leaving to immigrate to the United States. She had decided to sell off all her properties, including the one rented by Mooney, to a real estate developer. All tenants were required to vacate the premises by a certain deadline.

Just as Mooney was worrying about where she would move to next, other tenants from the neighborhood came to see her. "We have to band together and ask the landlord to compensate us for the relocation expenses" The tenants, unified and determined, in the end obtained compensation, and were all quite satisfied with it.

Mooney received a compensation of 17,000 MOP (Macau currency) from the owner of her villa. Back then, the average monthly income of a worker in Macau was around five to six hundred MOP. This sum was equivalent to a three-year salary. Using this money as a down payment, Mooney bought an apartment in a slightly more remote area, and at the same time, opened a small restaurant specialized in fried noodles in the vicinity. Her older daughter Xizhi helped her in the restaurant, and her son Zhiqiang, worked on a construction site as a wrought iron worker to earn a little more money.

Unfortunately, Mooney's restaurant didn't fare as expected, and it was a tiring business. A year later she sold the restaurant and returned with her daughter to work at the garment factory, sewing was always what she preferred.

Quan and Mooney's two eldest sons, Liu Zhiwen and Liu Zhiwu were settled in Hong Kong. They would only come to Macau to visit their mother during the Chinese New Year Holiday or during some other special events, the whole family rarely reunited.

Macau's economy in the 1980's was sluggish and couldn't be compared to that of Hong Kong, even though the latter was just on the other side of the same river. For a lot of young people who had immigrated to Macau from the Chinese mainland, there seemed to be no "hope" there. So, in search of a better life, a good portion of them smuggled themselves from Macau to Hong Kong hiding in small fishing boats.

Seeing as all their friends were leaving Macau for Hong Kong, Liu Zhiqiang and Liu Xizhi, perplexed, didn't know what to do. Zhiqiang decided to return to

Indonesia to work with his father. Wenquan hoped that his youngest son could inherit his businesses. While the timid Liu Xizhi for her part, didn't have the guts to sneak into Hong Kong. Someone introduced her to a Vietnamese overseas Chinese who lived in Hong Kong, and she didn't even wait to get to know him before she rashly married herself to him. Afterwards, she applied for her mother and her younger sister Xilian to move to Hong Kong. While Liu Zhiqiang for his part, after living in Indonesia for two years, decided to return to Macau.

13. Lie Low, and Stay Put?

I've always wanted to know my father's identity. As far as I can remember, my father's whereabouts were always very erratic. When he passed away, his funeral was held in the Funeral Parlor in Hong Kong named "International". A great many relatives and friends came to bid farewell to my father, there were also quite a few strangers. The wreaths of flowers brought on by visitors filled the mourning hall to capacity. Among them, a big one had a message attached that read "Dear Mr. Liu Wen Quan, rest in peace, the People's Republic of China's State Council sends its condolences."

If my father had been just a small regular businessman, why would he have received a wreath of flowers of condolences from China's central government?

Dismissing his wife's and children's countless pleas, Liu Wen Quan had always refused to join them to live in Hong Kong or Macau. He would always turn them down saying he still had unfinished business in Indonesia. Sometimes, he would also mysteriously tell them that: "Premier Zhou (Prime minister of China from 1949 to 1976) wants me to stay put in Indonesia."

Years went by and the day came when my father fell seriously ill. Faced with no other options, he finally agreed to let his children vouch for him so that he could obtain a visa to come live in Hong Kong. During the festivities of the Chinese New Year of 1984, my father's request for a residence visa in Hong Kong was approved. He did not hold on however till he could get his Hong Kong residency identity card, on that very day, he drew his last breath. On his death bed, he was continuously muttering, "I must go to Beijing next spring, for an important meeting"

On two different occasions in Indonesia, my father was arrested by the local government. The whole experience was extremely trying both times. One of these two arrests was made in Medan, my father had been profiled as a pro-communist and was arrested and imprisoned. With every sunrise there, guards would come in and escort fellow prisoners out to be executed. My father had resigned himself to his terrible fate. One day, unexpectedly, a young army officer came in and singled out my father for questioning. The officer ordered my father to look up at him, and asked if he knew him. The officer looked familiar to my father, but he feared the question to be a trap, so he dared not answer it too directly. It turned out that this young Indonesian officer was also from Medan. As a teenager, he was poverty-stricken and would often go hungry. Whenever he starved too much, he went to a nearby Chinese-run grocery store where there was a gentle "Nyonya" (a honorific term to refer a married foreign woman) who used to give him water and some food.

"These are very good people, a good family, honest in business, they're really not the kind who would foment trouble for the government." The officer said. The grocery store owner he was referring to be my father, and the Nyonya was my grandmother. To repay the my grandmother for her kindness and care toward him when he was young, the Indonesian officer released my father.

After the Second World War, both the Netherlands and Japan no longer ruled over Indonesia. Indonesia declared its independence, and Sukarno became Indonesia's first president. The newly independent country established diplomatic relations with China soon after the founding of the New China, and the interactions between the two governments and both countries' private sectors were frequent. At that time, Wen Quan began to work for the Chinese Consulate. As a young overseas Chinese leader, he was mainly responsible for receiving government officials from China and co-organizing the consulate's activities. He was also a shareholder of several local overseas Chinese newspapers. He participated in various associations and was very active in his community.

Up until the late 1950s, the international political situation was very unstable. The Indonesian military was secretly plotting a coup d'état, and incited anti-Chinese sentiments among the populace. They regularly arrested Indonesians deemed Communists, and the shops of Chinese people doing business in Indonesia were often the target of vandalism and looting. At the same time, several anti-Chinese regulations were implemented. Because the Chinese in Indonesia generally didn't apply for citizenship, the government ruled that the Chinese who had not naturalized in Indonesia could not own a business, and all Chinese schools were forced to close as well. The living conditions had become quite poor for the Chinese in Indonesia. Everyone wanted to flee the country. Among those Chinese who were planning to leave, there were two groups divided along political lines. One group supported the Nationalist Party (Guomindang) and wanted to go to Taiwan, and the other group supported the Communist Party (Gongchandang) and preferred the Chinese mainland. Those who supported the Nationalist Party of Taiwan (Guomindang), were called the "blue asses", and those who supported the Communist Party of mainland China were called the "red asses." There was constant fighting between the blue and the red and the main purpose of this strife was to seize leadership of the local overseas Chinese association.

In the early 1960s, my father actively worked in conjunction with the Chinese government on the repatriation of overseas Chinese living in Indonesia. His main job was the distribution of the repatriation application forms. During that period, the Chinese government brought back to the mainland about 100,000 Indonesian overseas Chinese.

14. The Fate of Water

The year her father passed away, Xilian was 22 years old. She had already graduated from university and had been working in a Chinese company for two years. After completing her secondary school in Macau, Xilian wanted to continue studying at university. Xilian had always loved studying, but after being robbed and looted for years, her father's businesses in Indonesia no longer allowed her family to afford her tuition in a Hong-Kong based university and even less so in a foreign institution.

That same year, the Chinese government was nearing 30 years of self-imposed isolation from the outside world. After chairman Mao Zedong breathed his last, the decision was taken for China to gradually open to the world. In 1978, Jinan University, a mainland Chinese university who had a long history of accepting overseas Chinese students, began to recruit overseas and Hong Kong and Macau based students. This was seen as very good news by Xilian and her classmates who applied for the entrance examination. Not long after passing the exam, Xilian received her admission letter.

When Xilian's mother learned that her daughter was planning to study in Guangzhou (Mainland China), she got nervous and uneasy. She had just finally succeeded in bringing back her four other children from China, where they had gone to study, and then merely a few years later her youngest daughter wanted to go to China to study as well, as if there was no escaping this fate in her family. Mooney was scared and preoccupied, so she thought she should ask the gods for guidance. She ran to Hong Kong's Wong Tai Sin Temple, a Taoist temple, where she drew lots to obtain answers to her questions from the gods. She received the stick No. 22, titled "A young girl's longing", the associated poem went like this:

The autumn waters are flowing,
each in its own direction.
The hatred is long and deep.
I wonder who I can rely on
to express my longing.
I am so sad that I am heartbroken.

Mooney found an interpreter in the temple with whom she was acquainted and asked him to interpret this poem she had just received. The man told her that this was one of the worst sticks to receive, a bad omen. He said that if she had received this answer from the gods as a response to a question, she had formulated about herself, it was cause for worry and insecurity. If her question was about a trip, it meant the person about to depart on this trip was going to be met with a great deal of disaster and adversity. "Your daughter definitely shouldn't go. With such an omen, I fear her departure could lead your family to ruin and it could even attract death to your doorstep. "

Mooney tried all she could to stop her, but it would prove impossible to turn her daughter around, she was determined. In the end, Mooney resigned herself to her departure and prepared her daughter's luggage. Around that time, Xilian had asked for a bicycle, but Mooney couldn't spare the money for it. It shamed her that she couldn't afford even that for her daughter. To see her daughter be disadvantaged was heartrending. By the time she was born, the family's fortune had already declined, and she did not get to enjoy the good days like her brothers and sister did. Xilian was born 11 years after Mooney had had her youngest child. Before this child however, Mooney had resorted to abortion on several occasions, using medicinal herbs. Xilian was unexpected and Mooney had used abortion drugs continuously till the third month of pregnancy. But Xilian wouldn't go, she was a tough one. Then one night, Mooney had a dream where her mother Luo Mei was holding a small baby in her arms, this little baby had lost its hairs and had a scrawny and deathly pale face. Luo Mei visibly enraged told Mooney with a fierce tone: "You should stop taking your medicine, it's poison, look what you're doing to your baby!" Mooney woke up with a gasp, from that moment on, she stopped taking the abortion medicine. When Mooney gave birth to Xilian, she was 36 years old. At that time in China, 36-year-old women rarely had children. It was shameful for a woman of that age to still engage in sexual intercourse, it was seen to provide undue distraction for the woman's husband. Mooney felt ashamed, and to avoid disapproving looks and whispers, she stopped going out and hid at home for nine months.

In time, Liu Wen Quan and Mooney accompanied their youngest daughter Xilian to register at Guangzhou's Jinan University. Wen Quan also took her daughter to the local bank, where the bank manager, after having welcomed them, explained to Xilian that with the arrangements taken, she could come at the bank on the first day of every month to draw a sum of fifty RMB, to cover for her living expenses. For her first year in university, in addition to new clothes, Xilian received as a gift from her parents a Phoenix bicycle, a Seagull camera, and finally, her father invited her and her classmates for a hearty meal at the luxury Huaqiao Hotel in Guangzhou.

Fifty RMB back then (late 70's) was a large sum. An average worker's salary was only about 36 RMB. In China, it was the so-called "Do your job, get thirty-six, don't do it, get thirty-six anyway" era.

Xilian lived comfortably on her monthly 50 RMB stipend. Not only did she not need apply for scholarships and grants like the other students, she could also set some aside for the summertime trips she did all around the country. When she graduated after four years of study, the allowance ended. Xilian once asked the bank manager about the source of these funds. The manager's response was that it was a small sum of money that Mr. Liu had put aside decades ago. The interests compounded over this long period of time, and the sum was now more than enough to cover for Xilian's studies expenses. At first, the explanation seemed plausible. Xilian didn't ask herself how to come the whole sum conveniently corresponded to exactly just forty-eight months of living expenses. She didn't wonder either why she did not have to sign anywhere upon collecting the funds at the bank or even how her parents, who had been ostensibly in dire financial straits for a while, were suddenly able to be so generous to her in terms of financial help and gifts.

It wasn't until recently, decades later, that an old friend of Liu Wen Quan told Xilian that these four-years of living expenses had been arranged by "the organization." It was a common name for the central government.

Xilian successfully completed her four-years study program at Jinan University, and it all went without a hitch. There was no catastrophe, such as had been predicted at the Wong Tai Sin temple. The family did not end up in ruins and no one died, Xilian simply returned to Hong Kong.

That year, the students returning to Hong Kong and Macau from Jinan University were the first group of graduates to do so after the reopening of the university to foreign students. A placement service administered by the Chinese government was available to them in Hong Kong, so they could be immediately assigned to a position related to their field of study. Xilian was assigned to a branch of a Chinese Hi-Tech company named "China Resources", where she worked as assistant manager of the human resources department.

The early days of one's career are one of life's many trials. Xilian's manager was a woman who had graduated from Hong Kong's Baptist University, and she scornfully looked down on those who had graduated from the Chinese mainland's universities. She mocked them for using the placement program of the Chinese government and wouldn't miss an occasion to remind them that they had relied on the connections of "Grand Pa" (aka Chinese Government) to get a job. Four years later, for some unknown reasons, the company decided to fire this woman. The President of the company wanted Xilian to be the one to prepare the termination letter. The plan was for Xilian to take over the human resources department in her stead. When Xilian handed over the letter to said woman, she looked Xilian in the face contemptuously, and told her in a spiteful tone, "You finally got what you always wanted." Xilian did not argue with her, she did not respond, she stomached it. Xilian took over her job the best she could, and a month later, unhesitatingly resigned.

15. My hometown

In 2004, my mother took me along with my older brothers and sisters on a trip back to the city of Medan in Indonesia to visit our relatives.

Although Mooney's youngest brother was happy to see his sister, whom he hadn't seen in years, he dared not speak much to her. He just silently sat beside her with a smile on his face. His daughters were gentle and polite to him, as if he had been a guest in their house. His only son however wouldn't even throw a glance at him. A mere few words from my uncle would cause his son's facial expression to immediately turn into a mix of contempt and scorn. Of course, there were motives for such hatred.

Mooney's young brother's wife had given him several children, and when they were young, the family's poverty made their life difficult. That wouldn't stop my uncle however from engaging in all sorts of romantic adventures. He spent a lot of time outside the house courting ladies and his conquests were numerous. From widows to young students, some of them Chinese, other Malaysians, and some others from even more exotic places, the love stories never stopped. The subsistence of the whole family depended entirely on his wife, my hardworking, virtuous and responsible auntie.

When the children grew up, they were able to work, and the situation of the family took a turn for the better. My uncle's young son turned out to be the most successful. He opened a large chicken processing factory in Jakarta, it produced chicken meat, eggs and even brushes made with the chicken's feathers, nothing was wasted from the animals. Nonetheless, this son hated his father the most. We were in the same room once when he learned that his father had "married" a teenage Indonesian girl the year before, and he then came very close to resorting to violence against his father. His sisters stopped him in the act just as he was losing it. He slammed hardly on the table and yelled and cursed, so his sisters told him: "Let's think of this girl as domestic help hired to take care of our father, that way, our mother won't have to toil so hard to do all the chores, isn't that a good deal?"

Unwillingly, he contained his rage and calmed down.

Mooney's older brother and second brother, along with all three of her sisters had all passed away. Only her third brother was still living in his old house by the sea, where he still had his Chinese medicine clinic. He was still telling his patients about his father's encounter with the Goddess Guanyin and how his curing powers were derived from the gods. He was a popular and renowned doctor in the area, and some wealthy patients flew all the way from Jakarta to seek his medical treatments.

Mooney's relatives who had stayed in Indonesia, were much like these calm and peaceful oxbow lakes left behind by the current, they hadn't gone to a thousand places to look for the ocean. Their children had already lost their native language and couldn't speak more than a few words of Chinese. They stayed there diligently working, and even though it was for lack of a better option back then, they eventually made a good life for themselves.

In 2005, my mother took us back to my father's hometown in Shanwei. There, the second brother of my father had four sons and four daughters. All his daughters were married and had moved out of the house. My uncle and his wife lived with their four sons, their son's children, and the children of their children. They still lived in the house that my parents had bought there decades ago.

It is said that after my father died, my youngest uncle disappeared. He hadn't contacted any members of our family for years and no one had any idea about his potential whereabouts.

My father's older sister still lived in the area. Her family lived off fishing and they had had a poor and hard life.

The youngest sister of my father had moved with her family to the nearby city of Zhuhai, close to Macau. Her husband died of cancer at a young age, but since he had bought some properties before leaving them, she could still live independently and comfortably with her family.

Every time my mother would visit the members of her husband's family still living in their hometown in mainland China, they all seemed restless and uncertain. My younger uncle and his wife would always raise the subject of the renovation of the tombs of their ancestors. They saw the Liu family's situation and circumstances as having been wretched for a long time. Their family always had to move around looking for work, they had been constantly drifting. In their mind, it must all have been because they hadn't built a decent enough resting place for their ancestors, because they hadn't honored them as they should have.

Throughout the entire year of 2017, I had to keep travelling back and forth from Asia to North America to follow my spouse in his work assignments. Whenever I returned to Canada, I couldn't help but revel in that country's incredible safety and peacefulness. That year, both my parents had already passed away, and their past had gone with the wind as well. Generations W, or X, or Y, Z, have their differences, but in the end, they're all very much the same. What's the real identity of my father? Was my mother brought down from the skies to my father by the Goddess Guanyin? None of it really matters anymore, what matters is that the story of our present generation continues, and the story of the next generation is just beginning. If one day, finally, I cease to drift all over the world, I wish to become like one of these oxbow lakes, to stop flowing and to finally find my resting place here in Canada, where I hope to stay forever.

Thunder from the South of the Cloud

IN A SMALL Burmese village bordering Yunnan Province of China. On a certain day of November 1960, the usual sweltering heat of that region was as present as ever. The heatwave caused a kind of yellowish hazy smoke to emanate from the ground and gush straight to the sky where it mixed and intertwined with the clouds forming a kind of dirty smog.

A few peasants could vaguely be seen working in the rice fields that surrounded the village, a woman of short stature rested with her three children by the edge of one of the rice paddies.

This woman went to the field every day as part of her work. Her main duty was to bring the field workers their daily lunch. She worked as a domestic helper for the local landlord, a Burmese family. Her employer was good to her, the lodging and meals were free for herself and her three children. She had always felt very grateful for it. Many other women who found themselves in the situation where she had once been, had to resort to selling their bodies to provide for their subsistence, so she considered herself quite lucky to be able to serve as a domestic helper.

One night at dusk, the landlord sternly commanded her to bring all her children to the rice paddy first thing come dawn. She didn't argue or question the order. She remembered receiving a similar command two years ago and knew from experience that something significant was going to happen. She was a firm and persistent woman and had always had faith in her family's destiny and good fortune. She didn't expect to see her days slowly meet their end in this remote Burmese backcountry but rather longed to return one day to her husband's side.

Come morning, the woman and her children were quietly sitting in the field. Her children had accompanied her to the rice paddy every day for the past few years and the sun had given them a dark tan and the work had made them sturdy for their age. They knew and understood their mother's difficulty and were therefore very obedient and helpful. For the day's occasion, they were all dressed in their best clothes, all neat and tidy. The mother had combed her long hair into a bun which she had skewered with a silver pin.

Suddenly, a protracted thunderous sound reverberated through the sky. A strong wind blew all over the field and the sun-dried gritty sand beneath them rose up to form a whirlwind of dust that blinded the children who could barely keep their eyes open. As the thunder grew louder, the little woman looked up and saw an approaching thick flock of what she first thought were “large birds”. It appears the time had come. She did not run away, and the other laborers present around her likewise remained in place.

The “large birds” were getting closer, and with them the “thunder” was getting louder. The woman then realized that these were not birds but airplanes, more specifically warplanes. She tried to count them: one, two, three, four, but the swirl of sandy dust the planes raised wouldn’t let her see how many of them were approaching.

They landed nearby on the field where they could be seen by the woman and the other workers. The pilots were soldiers, in full combat gear, and they began to energetically wave their hands toward the group. The peasants vacillated as they pondered their options, whilst the woman picked up her toddler and shouted to her two oldest: “Run! We are going to see Dad.” She raced toward the planes in the field as tears of joy trickled down her cheeks. Her vision was blurry, but hope was just ahead. She hadn’t cried when faced with hardship and suffering, but before her salvation she couldn't hold back.

Finally, upon reaching the planes with her children, the soldiers took them one by one onto the planes. When her turn came, she hesitated. She looked back at the small village behind her that was now just at the other end of the purple-red colored cloud that hovered above them. It was hard for her to let go, but when the soldiers urged her to climb up the plane, she acquiesced and turned around.

The summer in Quebec is exceptionally beautiful. The weather remains relatively warm and isn't comparable to Asia's sultry summer-time heat. Various activities animate the cities to the great pleasure of both locals and tourists. Immigrants to Quebec like to invite their distant friends and relatives to come spend their summer holidays in this lovely province.

That year, two of my friends "Juan" and "Qian" had both, without prior communication between themselves, invited their parents to come to Canada. Juan's mother was coming over from Taiwan and Qian's parents flew in from Kunming, Mainland China.

Juan is from Taiwan, Qian is from Mainland China, I am from Hong Kong, and we are all Chinese.

On the first Sunday following the arrival of the three elders to Canada, they were taken to the church by their respective daughters for Sunday mass. Surprisingly, despite having sat for almost 20 hours on an airplane not long before and this being their first time in Canada, they were not at all tired and quite the contrary, were all vibrant with energy and enthusiasm.

Both families' seniors were led to seats on different sides of the church's main aisle, as everyone was chanting the hymns and reciting the lectures.

It was customary for the priest to welcome newcomers to the church before commencing his sermon, so the priest first introduced Ms. Chen Li Yu Ying, the mother of Juan from the beautiful and bountiful island of Taiwan. Mrs. Chen then slowly stood up and was seen at that moment by the father of my friend Qian who was sitting at the back of the other section of seats on the other side of the aisle. He could only see her from the back, but when he heard her name, his heart missed a beat.

The priest then introduced the parents of Qian from Yunnan, Mr. and Mrs. Shi Bin. Qian's mother then stood up with the support of her husband who stood up as well. Mrs. Chen turned around, and her eyes met those of Mr. Shi, the latter then excitedly murmured to his wife: "Sometimes in this world we are met by kind of incredible coincidences. It has been decades since we last saw her, and then we come upon each other in this distant foreign country."

From that moment, it was nearly impossible for the three of them to lend much attention to the preaching. They couldn't wait for the mass to end to finally meet again. When the service finally concluded, the father of Qian walked to Juan's mother with hurried steps. Mrs. Chen was already standing in the aisle next to her seat, ready to greet him.

Time had not altered them beyond recognition, Mr. Shi was as tall and hefty as he had been in his prime, and the petite Mrs. Chen had retained her calm and delicate composure. He no longer wore his knee-length military coat today, but she still combed her hair in a bun. He was visibly excited as he held both hands of Juan's mother, all these emotions that had revolved in him for what appeared to be centuries could finally be expressed. He could still vaguely remember that day fifty years ago, when she was leaving Yunnan, when all he could do was to silently watch her gentle silhouettes disappear in the forested mountain.

"Commander Shi, how are you?" Mrs. Chen spoke first.

"Mrs. Chen, we are fine. Isn't the Major General Chen accompanying you?"

"Unfortunately, not, he has already left this world." Mrs. Chen replied softly.

After the church service, Qian's parents invited Mrs. Chen for a home visit on her way back. Once arrived, the excitement had had time to gradually recede, and Mrs. Chen began to doubt the whole situation. She examined the old man in front of her and murmured,

"Are you really Commander Shi? How come you don't resemble him? I recall a thin and tall man."

Qian's father responded by taking Mrs. Chen to the mirror he had at his home entrance, and pointed at the small and thin old woman that stood by his side in the mirror saying:

"Take a good look, haven't your hair gone grey as well? Haven't you aged? How can you expect me to look the same after all these years? Of course, my appearance has changed." The argument was convincing, but the mood had soured a tad, nonetheless.

My friend Qian told me pretty much everything she knew about that evening. She said, "That night, the three of them talked for a very long time. Mrs. Chen opened a bottle of the Golden Gate Chinese sorghum she had brought with her from Taiwan. My father opened a bottle of Maotai wine, which he had preciously kept for a long time, expressly for special occasions. They drank a lot that night. They talked about the good old times, they high-fived and sang out of tone, from time to time they even had to hold back their tears, as they reminisced about the past."

Mrs. Chen humorously called this meeting "the gangster's summit". Back then, both sides of the armed conflict called each other 'bandits'. They did not expect to one day there is the reunite with the bandits from the other side, in Canada, several decades later.

Having grown up in Hong Kong, I never cared much about the particulars of China's wartime history. But when Qian began to tell me about it, she was so passionate and her descriptions were so colorful, it aroused my curiosity. I had to learn more about it, I wanted details. I dared not go straight to Mrs. Chen, she had just recently lost her husband, and I felt it would have been rude to go ask her questions on such a topic so directly.

So, I figured my best way forward was to ask Mr. Shi, Qian's father. I had made up my mind about visiting Mr. Shi, I wanted to listen to him tell me all about his wartime story from his own perspective. That's when Qian poured a bucket of cold water on my plan to visit her father.

"Even if you ask my father face to face, he'll find some excuse to not tell you anything. He'll say he doesn't remember this old stuff that it happened too long ago. Your best bet is to let me ask him for you."

Qian picked my curiosity even more. She said: "My father is a diligent and rigorous agent, the old-school type. When I was a child, as he returned home, he used to bring me bowls of delicious Yunnan rice noodles. My mother regularly asked him where he bought those, but my father would always just simply reply, "some place", he never gave any definite answer about anything. It's his professional instinct. Even for small, apparently trivial matters, my father won't give any more information than what is required. A person who has been trained as a spy and who has done this kind of work for a long time has this sort of vigilance ingrained in his bone marrow. It's become a solidly anchored habit, one that isn't going to change."

I wasn't going to give up that easily and so I kept asking my friend Qian to arrange a meeting for me with her father. My perseverance eventually paid off. When her father came over to Canada for his second visit, I got the opportunity to meet him.

It was in October, and the weather was getting cooler already. The meeting was arranged to take place at the big house of a good friend of Qian who was a rich new immigrant from China. The house was nestled by the Saint Laurent River and the view was gorgeous.

The daughter of Qian's friend had invited Qian's two beautiful and lovely children as well. She wanted to use them as models for a photography project she had been assigned in college.

When we arrived at the house, the kids and women went down to the basement to work on their important business, leaving me alone with Uncle Qian who was sitting by the window. I was prepared to be assailed by the questions of a suspicious man given the nature of the subject that interested me, but quite to my surprise, Mr. Shi simply asked me a little bit about my career and my background, and then quickly switched over to the main topic.

His story took place during the Chinese civil war, in the period that followed the Japanese capitulation of 1945, at the end of the Second World War. The fighting opposed the Kuomintang and the Communist Party of China, and the situation for the Kuomintang army was getting worse by the day. As the Kuomintang troops were retreating, mostly toward the island of Taiwan, a division (the Kuomintang army 93) could not reach the Taiwan island in time and was forced to retreat to the "Daluo Town" region of the Xishuangbanna area, in the southwestern Chinese province of Yunnan. They were waiting there for an order from the Kuomintang central government, as they thought an order to counterattack the Communist party would come imminently.

Juan's father was a Major General of the Kuomintang army 93 (called the national army at the time). He had taken with him his wife and his three children who were all less than 10 years old. Stationed with him in this small village on the border between China and Myanmar were a group of soldiers under his command. The Xishuangbanna was a poor rural place, and as it turned out, the national army never received any more help or assistance from the "Kuomintang central government", which no longer existed. No more orders or instructions would ever come.

They remained stranded there, forced to fend for themselves alone on this barren land, without legal status neither in China nor in Myanmar. Whenever they were not busy hunting or fishing, they had to face the constant harassment raids of the Burmese (Myanmar) army, along with the attacks of the drug lords of the area they were in, where eventually became known as the drug-producing region called the "Golden Triangle of southeast Asia".

A few years after the founding of the New China by the Communist Party. The People's Liberation Army (PLA) entered the Xishuangbanna area. Shi Bin served as a Commander for the Communist Army at that time. He was young; he had great military knowledge and led expeditions with skillful and professional soldiers by his side. He was also a Confucians scholar, who enjoyed playing the Chinese flute “xiao” in his spare time.

When he entered the Xishuangbanna area, he received a report from a subordinate describing the conditions of an isolated residual division of the Kuomintang army 93, currently hiding in “Da Luo”. He felt that even though these men were “enemy bandits”, they were also Chinese just like him, they shared the same culture and were of the same people. He learned that the men were still waging war on several fronts around them, that the wife of the commanding officer had brought with her other female relatives and children, that they had built a “school” in the countryside, and that they tried as much as possible to survive in harsh conditions. They weaved their own clothes and ploughed the land around them. Having been caught in a continuous and unending war for years on end, they still tried to live their life as normally as possible.

Given the circumstances and because Shi Bin had yet to receive an order regarding this remaining military division of the Kuomintang, he decided to leave things as they were and both sides lived peacefully for a time. But one day the order came, and Shi Bin dutifully led the attack on the Daluo Town. What was left of the Kuomintang army 93 was no match for the full force of the Communist military. The men of the national army fought to cover their retreat, and eventually made it over the border, into Myanmar. There was no way however for the women and children that accompanied them to follow through the fighting and running, so they were left behind. They were later captured by the Communist forces. That is how Juan's mother, Mrs. Chen, became a prisoner of war.

Shi Bin had heard about the Major General Chen's wife, he knew she was kind, knowledgeable and well educated. She had always done her outmost to help the relatives of this group of unfortunate soldiers. He held her in high regard and always treated her with courtesy.

He had not interrogated her in a formal face-to-face meeting, but they met each other when he toured the prisoners-of-war camp. Juan's mother had a good impression and a good feeling about this young officer. He was polite, handsome, educated and looked brilliant.

While the 93rd division of the National Army was stuck in Myanmar, their families were detained on the border with the Chinese province of Yunnan. Shi Bin, on the one hand, was responsible for the welfare of this large group of prisoners, but on the other, he had to make sure they would not be able to help a potential counterattack of the Kuomintang army. He couldn't let down his guard.

One morning, Shi Bin received a top-secret telegram. He carefully read its content several times over, and then burned it. When all that was left of it were ashes, Shi Bin checked the service pistol he wore on his belt, and then immediately went to the kitchen to ask for the leftover steamed buns from yesterday. He took out two pairs of unused clean socks from his suitcase, all the cash he had on him plus two silver coins and stuffed everything into an envelope.

Under cover of night, dressed in his military uniform, Shi Bin gathered everything he had prepared, and began to walk rapidly toward the prisoners-of-war camp. After fifteen minutes at a hurried pace, Shi Bin's face had reddened, he was nervous and restless.

Just when Mrs. Chen, Juan's mother and the wife of the Kuomintang Major General Chen, had just put to bed her three young children in accordance with the rigorous schedule they followed, and just as she had picked up her book to begin her before-bed reading, a rapid and unnerving knock on the door resounded through the room. She got up and opened the door prudently, Shi Bin was standing alone on her doorstep, and he slipped into the room and immediately closed the door. Mrs. Chen was scared and shocked and apprehensively looked at him for a moment. Fortunately, Shi Bin didn't look like he had come there to enjoy himself. He was carrying a large bag and looked rather serious, so she breathed a sigh of relief.

"Hurry up and pick up your stuff, I'm taking you and your children over the border tonight" Shi Bin said.

"I've brought some food for you in this bag, just take what you really need here. Once you arrive in Myanmar, you'll be picked up."

She did not argue with Shi Bin's "order" whatsoever. She entirely trusted the young man. Shi Bin stood by and watched her, as she pulled her long black hair and wrung them into a bun, before pricking them with a silver pin. She then began to gather her clothes and effects from all over the room, she was packing everything in such a quick and orderly manner, it was as if she had been waiting for that day for a long time and was already prepared. She hesitated when she looked at the bamboo flute on the table, she didn't think she need it.

Shi Bin saw her hesitate about the flute and told her: "Take it with you, when you get over the border, you'll just have to blow a few notes through it and I'll know you're safe." Just as he said that he realized that he wouldn't hear the flute anyway, since she would have to cross over a mountain to traverse the border and she would be too far away to be heard. Moreover, she was fleeing at nighttime in panic with three children, how could he expect her to just stop to quietly start playing the flute, he felt embarrassed.

Shi Bin picked up one of the three little children and strapped him to his back while he was still asleep. He held the oldest one by the hand and in his other hand, he carried two bags of effects. Mrs. Chen carried her little baby all swaddled in her arms, it was my friend Juan, and she was three months old.

The five of them began to make their way through the jungle at night. The path was difficult, they were moving slowly. They didn't dare speak or make any noise whatsoever. They walked along a mountain trail that led toward Myanmar.

After walking for almost two hours, they finally reached a small village. Shi Bin then told Mrs. Chen: "This is as far as I can take you". He gave her a detailed description of the direction, woke up the child on his back, and handed the two bags he held to the oldest child.

Juan's mother bowed reverently to Shi Bin and resolutely walked away with her three children. She didn't look back. Bin stayed there standing, agape, as he watched this gracious woman disappear through the jungle. He waited till he was sure they were far away and then fired a few shots toward the sky. The gunshots broke the peacefulness of this small village's early morning, and resembled a signal given to someone else, to report a mission accomplished.

To my surprise, when I interviewed Commander Shi, he spoke at length about his wartime memories, and he was generous with details. In a burst of excitement, I asked him: "Why did you go to such an extent to orchestrate the escape of the family of an enemy officer? Was the Major General Chen an undercover agent for the Communists?" However, the question was untimely and inappropriate, and I immediately regretted asking it. Did I really need to know that? Qian had told me that she had already asked her father the same question, and it only made him angry. He scolded her for bringing up what she said was nonsense. He didn't want to slander the reputation of the Major General Chen, who had had an admirable and honorable military career within the ranks of the National Army.

I was lucky however, Mr. Shi did not take offense to my question, he just shook his head and responded with a firm "No".

I looked outside through the window, as a gentle gust of wind blew and whirled the tinted autumn leaves that rested on the grass in a spiral. I watched as two leaves of different colors danced gracefully in the air pursuing one another before diving back down to the ground.

What happened to Mrs. Chen and her children after they crossed the border into Myanmar? To that question Commander Shi responded that even himself didn't have a clear answer.

A few days later, I organized for my friend Qian to come meet me and my friend Juan at Juan's house. We both longed to discover what had happened to Mrs. Chen after she had fled Yunnan. Juan began her mother's story with the following: "My mother was a fierce woman. My father had always been quite submissive to her. No matter how unreasonable she was, whatever fit of temper she'd have, my father would always tolerate it, he'd never protest or grumble. For myself and my siblings, it was utterly incomprehensible."

She also said that her father told her once that when he saw his frail delicate wife with her three young children come out of the crowd that day, returning to his side safe and sound after everything that had happened, he swore to heaven, that no matter how much hardship he'd face in the future, he would always honor, love and care for this woman, that he would always protect his family, for it was a miracle that he could still be there to do so.

In 1960, Taiwan was controlled by the Kuomintang, in exile from Mainland China after losing the war. The then government of Taiwan run by Chiang Kai-shek had no plans for the repatriation of the remnants of the National Army no. 93 and their relatives stranded on the Yunnan border with Myanmar, for all intent and purpose they had been abandoned. However, around that time, the Taiwanese government was under pressure to rescue its stranded soldiers and their families from the US government, who acted based on humanitarian principles.

In November 1960, a series of evacuation operations were carried out secretly under the guise of military exercises. The Kuomintang military aircrafts, who were operating under what was called the "National Thunder Military Exercises", rescued more than 4,000 family members of the National Army on the Myanmar side of the border with the Chinese province of Yunnan.

After the evacuations were over and all the relatives of the soldiers of the National Army who could be rescued had been transported to Taiwan, a great banquet was organized on the military base for the reunion of the families. The wife of the head of the government, Soong My-Ling personally presided over the welcoming celebrations. Thousands of soldiers who had been already in exile for several years in Taiwan had come to believe that they would never again hear from or see their wives and children in this life, that they were lost to them forever. Suddenly, the government was inviting them to a banquet to come find and pick up their families brought over from Mainland China. I couldn't claim to be able to put in writing the intensity of the emotion they felt.

Juan's father, emaciated and attenuated by years of grief and worry for his forsaken family, found his wife and his children among the multitude at the banquet that night. That is when he made his sacred vow to love and protect his wife at all costs for the rest of his life. When you live the miracle of being reunited with your lost family, you realize that nothing in the world matters more than your loved ones.

The Chen family started a new life in Taiwan. Mr. Chen left the army and became a bank employee. He never again spoke of his military past with anyone. His daughter Juan and her husband opened a trading business in Taiwan, they put much effort in it and it grew along the years, until they later immigrated to Canada.

Qian's husband, Commander Shi's son-in-law, studied the French language in a university in Mainland China, and they too, later immigrated to Canada, hoping for a better life.

Just as I was writing this story, one of my friends from university coincidentally sent me some photos of his trip to the Yunnan border. The pictures were taken in the small, beautiful village he visited, at an altitude of 1800 meters. You could see there was a quaint little chapel, and two massive mountains right next to it. "On the other side of these mountains is Myanmar," he said.

Could this be the place, where this story unfolded? In those turbulent times, the clouds in the sky kept drifting, and no one knew what the next one would bring, be it a furious tempest, or a gentle spring breeze.

Don't Be too Sentimental

SINCE FEI IMMIGRATED to Montreal, time seemed to have accelerated, and in a blink of an eye, she had spend fifteen years there. During the first few years, she kept herself busy studying. She spent the first two years in language classes, and then began to study accounting. However, two years later she realized that she was not interested in numbers at all, and no matter how hard she tried to keep at it, she felt there was no way she could hold on till graduation.

Fei gave up on her accounting course and began to work part time odd jobs. It didn't take too long however until a friend of hers who was working in a garment factory told her that the garment factory in the Chabanel District was recruiting. Even those with minimal experience could be considered. "If you can work with the diagrams and plans for making the clothes, you'll be an interesting candidate, you won't have any trouble finding a job."

After being introduced by her friend, Fei was hired as an order clerk in a large garment factory owned by a Jewish family. While she was working there, she spent her evenings studying sewing and design at the La Salle College. The Jewish owner liked the hard-working Chinese. Since Fei had immigrated to Montreal, time seemed to have accelerated, and in a blink of an eye, she had spent there fifteen years. During the first few years, she kept herself busy studying. She spent the first two years in language classes, and then began to study accounting. However, two years later she realized that she was not interested in numbers at all, and no matter how hard she tried to keep at it, she felt there was no way she could hold on till graduation.

Fei gave up on her accounting course and began to work part time odd jobs. It didn't take too long however until a friend of hers who was working in a garment factory told her that the garment factory in the Chabanel District was recruiting. Even those with minimal experience could be considered. "If you can work with the diagrams and plans for making the clothes, you'll be an interesting candidate, you won't have any trouble finding a job."

After being introduced by her friend, Fei was hired as an order clerk in a large garment factory owned by a Jewish family. While she was working there, she spent her evenings studying sewing and design at the La Salle College. The Jewish owner liked the hard-working Chinese. Fei was eager to learn and made quick progress and the boss held her in high regard. Soon, she was promoted from ordinary clerk to foreman.

One day, the factory owner's eldest son came up with the idea of establishing a factory in Asia. That way, their products could be sold directly on the Chinese market without having to go through extensive transportation. The first step in that project was to find someone willing to go live there for a time, to start-up the project. The area he had in mind was the province of Guangdong in China, where there were many factories from all over the world.

He first decided to approach Chinese male employees of his father's factory who had been working there for a few years. The project was discussed, and several men were somewhat tempted by the idea. However, when they returned home and discussed it with their wives, it was in all cases roundly rejected. The justifications were the same from everyone: the children were still too young and were still studying; the husbands moving to Asia would mean more income, but also more expenses; wives couldn't take care of both the old parents and the kids at the same time all by themselves. But the most important, and untold reason, was undoubtedly that the women didn't want to see their husband leave alone for Asia, where they'd be surrounded by a world of temptations, and they'd be put to the test. They didn't want to take the risk of losing their husbands for no good reason whatsoever. They had heard stories about those men who returned to China for "business", 99% of them let themselves be seduced over there. Few families could survive the husband leaving overseas for a prolonged period, seven to eight out of ten would eventually disintegrate.

The factory owner's son was then left with no other choice but to ask Fei. He knew Fei was single, that she didn't have family engagements would make her own decision without any distortion. He figured she would probably accept the offer without having to give it too much thought, and sure enough, Fei quickly and happily accepted the assignment.

The mere thought of returning to the lively and colorful Asian continent made her heart flutter. Canada was too dull for her; the so-called quality of life that people always referred to was trivial non-sense to her. What she needed first and foremost was for her spirit to find a resting place, free of worries, and to live with her heart wide open, to let her emotions out whenever they surfaced, and she felt Asia was just the place where she could do that at that point in her life.

When Fei landed in Shenzhen, she settled down at the Marriott Hotel. It is a five-star hotel, it is refined and comfortable, the personnel are polite and thoughtful, everything is being taken care of, Fei felt just like home.

Shenzhen is a city of immigrants. Those who truly hail from the city are a minority in it. Most of the people living here however come from other parts of Mainland China. But there are also "real" immigrants who come from different western countries. These foreigners come to China to look for opportunities or simply out of curiosity.

To live in Shenzhen, one does not need to learn the local language, the Cantonese. Since the people there come from all over the country, they all speak different Chinese dialects and sometimes, they just don't understand each other. For this reason, the Mandarin, China's official and common language, is widely used in the city. it makes everything easier. As Fei speaks Mandarin, there was no language barrier for her, she felt like a fish in water in Shenzhen.

When Fei arrived in Shenzhen, everything around her seemed new and exciting. Everything in the city is newly built and modern, there are skyscrapers as far as the eye can see. Inside each of these buildings there is a shopping mall, everything one might wish for is easily accessible. The warm maritime climate of the South convinced Fei that she had made the right choice, how could she ever regret escaping the cold and harsh Quebec winters at the company's expense?

Because Fei had signed for a long-term stay at the hotel, she had access to the hotel's VIP lounge. The lounge provided its guests with various simple refreshments and fresh fruits. But most importantly, there was a free open bar with all kinds of wines and beers. A strongly flavored American-style coffee was offered as well along with all sorts of sweets and desserts.

Fei quickly adapted to her new life in China. Her day-to-day social interactions however remained somewhat of a problem. She had been living in Montreal for years and she had gotten used to greeting the people she would encounter on her way.

At the hotel in the morning, when she came across other guests in the corridor for instance, Fei would smile and say good morning. Most of them though would not reply and they wouldn't smile back, they'd just look up at Fei in surprise, and then ignore her disdainfully before walking away in indifference. It disconcerted her every time.

Once, after a hard day of work, Fei went to the VIP lounge to cool off a bit. She was attended there by a young waitress who came to her table to gently ask her if she'd want a cup of coffee. Fei didn't even have time to formulate a reply when a neatly dressed man walked in. He was handsome and elegant, and when the waitress saw him, it was as if she had been struck by lightning. She instantly turned around toward him and left Fei behind unattended. She walked up to the gentleman with a smile and guided him to a seat by a window with all the care in the world. "I will bring you a pot of hot tea right away." The waitress told him. By that time, she had forgotten all about Fei.

Fei was a little upset, it appeared as though the men in this VIP lounge were entitled to a more dedicated service. She threw a mad glance at the gentleman by the window, just as he was looking in her direction. Their eyes met at that moment and the man didn't quite understand why that woman was looking at him with such an angry expression, but he nodded politely toward her with a little smile anyway, as he didn't how else to react.

Fei kept a disciplined daily routine when she was in Shenzhen. She got up at 8 o'clock in the morning, dressed and washed and then went down to the lounge to have breakfast. She then took a taxi to a meeting with a manufacturer, as she always had meetings planned with manufacturers, to discuss the possibilities of cooperation between both firms.

The men working for the local manufacturers in Guangdong (south of China) to this day still discriminated against women. Whenever the discussions touched the more specific and practical aspects of a potential cooperation, the factory managers remained vague and wouldn't respond anything of substance, they'd switch instead to more trivial subjects. To reach an agreement on anything, Fei had to call her boss in Montreal, without his symbolic approval of what had been discussed, the other party wouldn't move forward. These awkward situations kept happening repeatedly, and Fei felt dejected.

Fei usually finished her workdays between three and four o'clock in the afternoon. When she first arrived in Shenzhen, she liked to spend her weekends in Hong Kong. She didn't know anyone in Shenzhen, but she still had some old friends from her time in school over the border. There isn't much distance between Shenzhen and Hong Kong, but because the customs are always crowded, one still needs a few hours to make the trip back and forth. Fei had not seen most of her Hong-Kong friends in a few years, and they all had taken different paths in life. Everyone's interests had diverged, and the subjects of discussion had grown sparse. Time had rendered these old friendships brittle, and all that was left to enjoy were some simple greetings from time to time and occasional restaurant gatherings.

Fei is a sensitive and delicate woman; she speaks candidly and likes to express her views freely. She is joyful and welcoming and does not hesitate to share her glee with others, and even her own life experiences. Those who don't know her intimately could think that she likes to boast and show off for her extravagant ways.

Fei had a friend once who wasn't too fond of her manners, she hadn't gotten used to them, and she would often respond sarcastically and criticize Fei for the things she said or did. She was rude and gruff and more than once Fei ended up in tears.

Additionally, the restaurants in Hong Kong are incredibly expensive, a regular meal can end up costing more than five or six hundred Hong Kong dollars. Fei, who was used to budgeting when she lived her more humble life in Canada, oftentimes felt that it just wasn't worth it. For all these reasons, she went less and less to Hong Kong and eventually stopped altogether.

Every day after work, Fei was bored and lonely and had nothing better to do than to wander aimlessly around her hotel. There was a commercial street nearby with shops of all kinds. There were restaurants, clothing stores, hairdressers and so on.

Fei walked over there often and once entered a hairdresser salon that had a large and standard though attractive facade. The commerce was named Yong Qi. There always was a gathering of good-looking young girls in miniskirts at the door welcoming the guests.

The storekeepers are good at sizing up their clients, so when the receptionist saw the confused and uncertain expression on Fei's face upon entering, she knew she had to immediately send the manager to assist her. The "Manager" looked like a teenager, he wore a pair of perforated ripped jeans and a T-shirt imprinted with misspelled English writings. He wore a baseball cap sideward, and one couldn't miss his shiny stud earring.

The manager didn't talk much as he carefully worked on her hair for a little more than four hours. When he finally finished, Fei looked at the mirror in front of her and couldn't believe that she was looking at herself. She looked like a movie star with her beautiful wavy hair style. The crowd in the store couldn't stop admiring the result and complimenting Fei, and that increased her satisfaction even more.

As she was about to pay, the manager gently and affectionately said: "Sister, if you plan to come here often, it will be much cheaper for you to sign up for a membership card, you'll get a 50% discount on all our services." "Sister" is a term used in Mainland China to greet a woman with whom you have a close and warm relationship, regardless of the woman's age. Fei was touched that he'd call her sister in such a delicate way and obediently took out 3,000 yuan from her wallet to sign up for the 50% discount benefit card.

Fei returned to her hotel with her beautiful new hair blowing in the wind. Just as she stepped into the elevator, she was met face to face by the man she had seen in the VIP lounge earlier in the morning. The man stared at Fei for a good five seconds, no doubt taken by surprise by her drastic change of hair style, until Fei looked down toward the floor feeling visibly embarrassed. The man then realized he had been rude, so he said "Hi" to Fei, and introduced himself properly.

The man's name is Li Bin, he comes from California. He is the general manager of a high-tech electronics factory based in Shenzhen. He told Fei: "If you ever need help in Shenzhen, you can call me."

Fei wanted to make new friends in Shenzhen. So, in addition to joining a few interest clubs, she went to the "Yong Qi" hair dressing salon once a week. She also frequented a tea shop on the street corner beside her hotel, she liked to sip a few cups there regularly.

When she bought clothes, she liked to take them to a small sewing boutique located in a nearby narrow alley where a woman she affectionately called “Ayi”, or “auntie” in English, would make the necessary adjustments and alterations. She went there essentially just to have someone to chat with.

However, everyone in Shenzhen is very busy, they are trying to make a living and survive, so no one will waste time to exchange with you without a good reason. In the end, Fei didn’t have too much success making friends there.

Every day afterwards, Fei shared her breakfast with Li Bin. He’d always give her useful suggestions for her work. He also introduced her to some acquaintances he had whom he believed could be helpful to her. With his help, Fei’s work in Shenzhen made great progress.

Slowly and without realizing it entirely herself, Fei became dependent on Li Bin, both emotionally and professionally. She paid special attention to the absence of any ring on Li Bin’s left-handed ring finger, and she couldn’t suppress her excitement about the possibilities it entailed. Once, while in Li Bin’s presence, she saw a few young girls jealously looking at her, and whispering about her and Li Bin. She believed she heard them say that a certain Julie from the lobby came to see Li Bin in the afternoon the day before and brought him a bag of "Emperor Huang" fresh roasted chestnuts.

"Women make themselves pretty for those they love". Fei went to the beauty salon ever more often, she constantly recharged her discount card, so much that the 50% rebate was increased to 70%. In addition to the hairdressing, she also used the salon's other services, like facial treatments and massages.

The young girl who served Fei at the salon was named Ali. She was from the Sichuan region, and she had been transferred to this salon in Shenzhen from the head office of the company in Beijing. Ali was slim and slender, she had a small face, small eyes, a small nose, small ears, she was pretty and looked smart, a real gem.

Ali did a few 'facial' for Fei, and Fei liked her very much. She liked to listen to Ali's stories. She told Fei a little bit about herself, she said that her family was far away and that she had left them a long time ago, that she had been working different kind of jobs in various cities, all just to support herself and to be independent. Ali would also tell Fei stories about the strange people she had encountered while working, or some of the strange things that had happened to her.

Once, as Ali was massaging Fei, Ali said that she thought that the men in Shenzhen were better than the men from elsewhere in China, that at least they weren't too rough toward women. As they began to speak of how the men **treated** women, Ali began to feel aroused. She leaned over Fei as she was massaging her, while Fei, who was lying on the massage bed, began to feel excited as well. Fei looked up at the large mirror on the wall in front of her and saw that underneath the ultra-short mini skirt that Ali wore as part of her uniform, there was her flesh-colored thin stockings but no panties. Ali changed position and once more bowed down on Fei to massage her waist, that way Fei could feel her white, plump breasts rhythmically bouncing on her back.

During the Chinese New Year, Shenzhen's "immigrant" workers, who come from other parts of China, **will** return to their hometown to spend the new year holidays with their family. Most of them won't have other opportunities during the year to reunite with their close ones.

Fei had no plans to return to Canada during the holidays. It's Montreal's coldest season, and that's also when there are the most snowstorms. She preferred to go for a warmer climate, would she go to Sanya on the island of Hainan? Or to Bangkok in Thailand? Would she go alone, or should she look for someone to accompany her? Fei seemed to have got lost in wild and fanciful thoughts.

Come evening, Fei entered the VIP lounge to have supper, and she saw Li Bin there sitting at a table. A waiter who held an exquisite small velvet pouch in his hand was discussing with him. The waiter passed the bag on to a visibly excited Li Bin, who took a gold ring out from it. He then put the ring on his left hand's ring finger. He moved his hand in different directions as he examined the ring and nodded with satisfaction. He subsequently drew from his wallet two one-hundred-yuan red bills, which he used to pay the waiter.

After the transaction, Li Bin saw Fei standing at the entrance of the lounge, so he walked over to her. Fei looked at his ring and Li said: "The weather in the south is too hot and humid, it swells my fingers, so I asked a waiter here to help me get it to a jeweler who could loosen it a bit."

He then told Fei that in two days' time he would be headed back to the United States, to spend the holidays with his wife and children. He asked Fei if she had any plans for the holidays, and then he offered her his good wishes for the new year.

During the holidays, Fei went on a group tour of Southeast Asia. She got up early in the morning and followed the guide with the group till late at night every day. They'd stop at all the main attractions for a short moment, just to take a few pictures and then on to the next stop. Everyone in the group were with their spouse, or with their family. Fei was the single unaccompanied member of the group, and though lonely, no one took any special interest in her. It didn't affect her too much however, she enjoyed the calm, she just felt like being alone, with no one to trouble her thoughts, so she didn't try to reach out to anyone either.

The holidays passed quickly, and the day after Fei's return to Shenzhen, she was already back to work. As soon as she could, Fei went back to her favorite hair dressing salon. She was met by closed door however, padlocked with a big iron chain. She could see that inside of the shop, it was pitch dark. A large sign had been placed on one of the windows and it read: "This commerce is being renovated, will be back for business soon."

Fei knew all too well that this meant that the salon would never open again. She would never again see Ali and the young "manager", as well as the thousands of Yuan she had just deposited on her discount card, it was all gone.

Don't Go Further

AFTER LI BIN completed his bachelor's degree in Beijing university, he received a scholarship to study at the UCLA in the United States. He went there and completed both a master and doctoral degree. In 1989 he graduated, and because of the event in China that year, he was able to obtain his American permanent residency directly, no questions asked. He got married and had two children. In the span of ten years, he essentially went through most of life's biggest milestones.

Of course, building such a successful life is a step-by-step process. The day to day can still present its challenges and small setbacks are inevitable. With, nonetheless, Li Bin feels like his life of the past few years in North America has been quite stressful, to him it feels like he's just running around trying to cope by, his life is improving. Things are moving well, but while in the action he barely notices it. He has his wife at home, a son, and a daughter. His family's having it good, they live happily and comfortably. Li Bin is a grateful person, and he believes he owes all his "achievements" to his Cantonese wife. It appears to him that it is since the day he met her, that slowly and subtly her good luck began to influence him and on his life.

Li Bin's wife emigrated from Guangdong to the United States when she was 17 years old. Her father ran a small Chinese restaurant in Los Angeles, and she always worked there, she did not go to school, and she did not work elsewhere. Helping in her father's restaurant was all she had been doing in the United States ever since she had set foot there.

She was a typical Cantonese woman, more specifically, from the Chaozhou region of the Guangdong province of China. She was staunchly traditional and conservative. For the women of this region, it meant that as a girl she would submissively obey her father, as a wife it meant she would comply and acquiesce to her husband's wishes, and as a mother it meant she would heed and accede to her son's demands. To live by these principles was her existence's ultimate purpose.

She wasn't ugly but she never dressed well. She always wore loose shirts and ragged jeans. She had never even used make up and her complexion was grim and dull. For these reasons she looked much older than her actual age. Surprisingly however, none of it deterred Li Bin, his interest toward her was unimpeded, and he remained always good to her.

Li Bin's marriage was filled with love and respect, and it was approaching its 20th anniversary. He had never lost his temper with her, and he had never elevated his voice. Li Bin's inherent tender and gentle character was certainly to thank for that, but it was undoubtedly also because he believed that everything he had obtained in life, he had obtained because he had always benefited from his wife's support and good luck. A happy, rich and successful life is hard to come by, and for this reason it should be cherished.

When Li Bin first met his wife, he was just a poor foreign student, but she did not reject him for it and he would never forget that. When he ate at her father's restaurant, she always gave some extra meat for him. She did not accept his tips, and even offered him discounts. Their love wasn't a love at first sight kind of thing, it had developed over time because he had been at her father's restaurant almost every day for two years.

A few years later, through hard work, Li Bin managed to obtain a high-paying job in Silicon Valley. His family's quality of life was increased again by a notch. Right after he finished his Ph.D. at UCLA however, Li Bin couldn't find work suited to his qualifications. When he was still studying, he received a scholarship from the university but after graduating, all such payments were terminated. All he could rely on to make ends meet were occasional small jobs he obtained to install security and anti-theft systems for Chinese families.

Back in the early stages of their relationship, when the whole thing still looked quite uncertain and there were more questions than answers, it is Jie Ling, the humble and traditional Guangdong girl, who broke the ice and boldly took the first step. She told him that she had set aside enough to make a down payment on the purchase of a small house, but that she wasn't sure she would be able to support the monthly payments on the mortgage. She asked Li Bin to be her "tenant", that way, the rent he would have to pay anyway if he lived elsewhere could be used to allow her to afford her own house.

Li Bin had his wits about him, and he understood Jie Ling's intentions. Even though he was more accustomed to the girls from the north of China to their more casual and straightforward ways, he felt that the more gentle and supple temperament of a southern girl like Jie Ling would suit him better. Jie ling's general circumstances, her financial situation or career prospects, weren't as favorable as his own, but that didn't bother him at all, quite the opposite, it took pressure off him, it made him believe in the viability of a long-term relationship with her. He thought of the old saying: "A man stronger than his woman will be accompanied forever."

When there is a marriage, it is the tradition in Guangdong, in the south of China, for the groom or the groom's family to offer the bride's family a betrothal gift, otherwise known as the 'bride price'. The costs of the ceremony are also the responsibility of the suitor. Jie Ling's parents however wouldn't accept any gifts, and even offered to hold the wedding banquet at their own restaurant. Li Bin got to marry a good wife he loved, for free. He'd always remember the incredible kindness of Jie Ling's family, and he'd always be grateful for it.

Initially, when Li Bin brought up to his wife the subject of leaving his current employment to join his friend's company, Jie Ling protested. In the United States, they had finally joined the middle class, and letting her husband go to mainland China for work entailed risks she didn't want to take. But she knew men's restless hearts. From the expression of excitement that Li Bin had on his face every time he had a chance to travel for work, as if he was being freed from a cage, she knew she'd have to agree in the end with Li Bin's decision.

Li Bin told her: "I don't know how it's going to happen exactly, but just give me three years and you'll see; our family's fortune will rise." Li Bin then sought to reassure Jie Ling, saying that for him, family would always come first, and that he'd never do anything to jeopardize their family.

It was about two years ago, when Li Bin's former high school classmate Xu Zhiqiang gave him a call from Guangzhou. He told him that he had founded a high-tech electronics company in Shenzhen five years ago, and that the company had survived the most perilous first stages of existence. He believed it was now the time to move forward with the know-how and technologies they had developed, to begin to compete with the other high-tech companies that occupied the market. The company needed a leader, someone who had experience working overseas in a Fortune 500 company, to take up this challenge.

"I keep thinking about it and I believe you're by far the most qualified candidate. I've known you for many years, we've studied together, and you're a good friend. I really wish you could come and work with me to help me grow this company and make it successful."

Xu Zhiqiang painted a vivid picture of the future for Li Bin. He promised Li Bin that, were he to take up the position, he'd have free rein to manage the business as he saw fit. He'd simultaneously be responsible for the research and development of new products, as well as for their introduction to production. Xu hoped they'd be able to take the company up on the stock market in five years' time.

Li Bin knew Xu Zhiqiang was an ambitious man. He had already run several companies before. These companies had all done well, and Xu Zhiqiang had later sold them. He had earned enough money to ensure and that he, his children and even his grandchildren could enjoy a life of travel and leisure for times to come.

However, after a few years of playing golf, boredom got to old Xu and he grew increasingly restless, he had to do something.

With his networks, raising funds for a new venture didn't pose much of a challenge. Having so many resources right from the start had made this high-tech company a unique case. It was established in a prosperous and modern industrial area of Shenzhen, made successful by the succession of new business start-ups in the area, which reminded of the famous slogan: "Industry saves the country, hard work cheers the nation."

The day-to-day life in Shenzhen is at first incredibly exciting for those who move there. It's a young city, sprawling with an array of fledgling enterprises, that are unlike anything observable outside of mainland China. The new products developed by these companies are technologically extremely advanced and have generally an advance of at least three years over whatever is done elsewhere. These companies are unmatched in creativity and vitality. A simple visit to the Hua Qiang North shopping area to have a look at the technological products on display is enough to overwhelm Li Bin.

Li Bin is a gourmand and fortunately for him, there are as many restaurants in Shenzhen as there are stars in the sky. If you try a new restaurant every day, you won't eat the same meal twice for at least 6 months. It didn't take half a year however for Li Bin to grow weary of restauration, eating out every day had made him lose his appetite for it, and since he lived in a hotel, he couldn't cook his own meals, but much to his pleasure, the hotel had a VIP lounge for long-term guests where some basic western-style dining was offered. Most of lounge's guests were on business trips from abroad, and they generally shared a similar background, which made social interactions that much easier among them.

One morning, Li Bin, as usual, stepped into the lounge. He saw there that Julie, the assistant manager of the lobby's front desk, was attending a female guest. He had no idea as to why she had come to the lounge that day to service the guests.

When Julie saw Li Bin, she immediately turned toward him, ignoring the woman she was servicing, and approached him to greet him and take him to a table by the window.

Julie then told Li Bin that she had planned to go to the "Emperor" store that afternoon to buy some of the famous fried chestnuts that Li Bin so much adored. She told him she would bring them over to him after sunset.

Li Bin felt that Julie was overstepping boundaries with her "care" for him, and he inwardly reflected on how best to react. Li Bin then turned his gaze toward the other side of the lounge when he unexpectedly met the angry scowl of the female guest Julie had been attending just before him. Li Bin was astounded, he didn't know this woman. She was dressed neatly, like a genuine businesswoman, but she didn't look like she came from the mainland. He figured she must have been from abroad, and back in China on a business trip, so he responded to her furious glance with a little polite smile and a nod of the head.

Li Bin's new job at his friend's company is quite demanding, he is challenged at every turn. Aside from Xu Zhiqiang who is the main shareholder of the company, there are several other small and medium shareholders. There are among them individual investors but also institutional investors. Outside of China, foreign companies essentially only must concentrate on developing good products to achieve a long-term and stable growth. But in China, the market changes and evolves very quickly. It is often the case that a product won't have even made its way onto the market yet, that the company already must start working on the subsequent generation of the same product so as to not lose the interest of their customers.

The client is king, that's the country's golden rule. Customers believe that whatever is newer is better, and the companies have to adapt to meet client's wishes. Even if they lose money in the process, what matters most to them is to stay in the spotlight, to retain the market's attention.

Such irrational competition, coupled with the company's executives, who will often create internal challenges of their own by competing against each other, present quite a difficult work environment for Li Bin who is used to working in Western companies, where everything is planned and done step by step. In

Chinese companies, it is more of a "take one step, then think on the next step" short term approach. Li feels like he is pressured by everyone, the clients, the executives, the suppliers, and most importantly, just as he feels like he just can't adapt to this new environment, he also realizes that he is utterly helpless in changing the frenetic work culture that surrounds him.

After a busy day at work, Li Bin didn't feel like going out on the street for supper and went straight to the hotel lounge on the 15th floor instead. While waiting for the elevator, a beautiful woman with fluttering graceful hair walked toward the elevator as well, facing him. Li Bin had a good look at her and realized that it was the woman who had stared at him with an angry look in the lounge the other day.

After a few seconds spent looking at her fixedly, Li Bin realized he was being rude, so he immediately took the initiative to introduce himself. The woman didn't look like she was upset anymore, and the stage appeared set for a brighter start between the two. She introduced herself to Li, saying her name is Fei and that she came from Montreal, Canada. Both were from North America, and as it turned out, they were both generally interested in the same topics and shared similar opinions. They began to share their meals and chat together in the VIP lounge every day. Those who didn't know them could have easily thought that they were a couple.

Over time, Li Bin gave Fei many life and work suggestions and advice. Fei listened to Li and followed all his recommendations, which inevitably led Li to regard Fei's problems increasingly as his own.

In addition to Fei's growing dependence on him, Julie of the hotel's front desk showed herself to be increasingly enthusiastic toward Li Bin. She once told Li Bin that he was much like her father, and that she'd very much like to regard him as her "God father". Li Bin initially saw Julie as just a little girl, so he wasn't too careful with her and now he felt that they had gotten too close and intimate. She had become awkwardly devoted to him, like that day for instance, when she went to the 'Emperor' store, where she waited in line for a few hours just to get a bag of chestnuts for him. He later found out that the term "God father" in China could mean "Sugar Dad", so it then dawned on him that the whole situation had gotten out of hand and was outright inappropriate.

Fei wasn't like Julie, however. In her speech and actions, she hadn't given Li Bin any ambiguous hints of affection. The only thing was that she occasionally inexplicably blankly stared at Li Bin's left-handed ring finger. Li Bin, a cautious married man, had soon figured out from this what she had in mind.

Men and women are attracted to each other, and it is a phenomenon as old and natural as is the action of eating and breathing. During one's life it is inevitable that there will be encounters with persons of interest, the question is generally what then? Men are of course particularly fond of young women, and especially when it is the young women who take the initiative to approach them, how can they resist? Should they?

Li Bin is a father, a family man. Of course, he can feel the temptation, but he also knows that once this line is crossed, the joy is short-lived, and the troubles are long-lasting.

Li Bin always wore his wedding ring, but when he first arrived in Shenzhen, the climate was so warm and humid, it made his fingers swell and the ring wouldn't fit anymore. That's why he asked the waiter at the VIP lounge, Xiao Wang, to take his ring to a jewelry store that could adjust it for him. Therefore, for a time, his hands were freed from any signs of engagement, and many a girl mistakenly thought that they had in front of them a rich bachelor.

Li Bin already had enough problems at work, and it made it even more frustrating that he now had to deal with these delicate emotional issues on top of that.

He thought of being straightforward and go talk to these girls directly to make things clear, but he feared the girls would deny their feelings and say that it is he who misunderstood them, that he is making a fuss about trifles or that he sees love where there's nothing, basically that he imagined it all.

Li Bin expressly instructed Xiao Wang that day to deliver him the ring at the lounge during supper time. He knew that Fei would be present in the room, and Julie had also told him that she'd bring him something delicious to eat that night.

Li Bin put the repaired ring on his finger in the lounge and conspicuously turned his hand around a few times in the air with a happy expression. He took out two hundred yuan from his wallet and handed them over to Xiao Wang. He saw Fei by a table on the other side of the lounge and walked over to her. He then told her that he would be soon returning to the United States to celebrate Christmas with his family.

Fei remained polite and composed, her eyes drifted rapidly over Li Bin's ring finger and a slight expression of sadness made a quick and timid appearance on her face.

Li Bin noticed, and for a moment, he felt quite sorry for her. Just as he was about to say something to try to cheer her up, Julie entered the lounge. He foresaw the scene that was about to unfold before him, and he felt his heart pounding as a drop of sweat trickled down his forehead.

Purple

A purple flower
Without the sorrow of blue
Without the jubilation of red

The rain in the south
The snow in the north
The wind in the west
The sunrise in the east

Oh, old walls
New high-rises
Through countless streets and alleys
Heard the clip-clop of horse hooves
From that distant city
Comes the roar of war

Survive,
Death might be easier
Who believe in the reincarnation of life
After parting, who cannot meet again

Encounter in this moment
You raised me up
A heartbeat in life
Not only because of you
Please do not panic
Just close your eyes
And dreaming with that purple flower.

Acknowledgement

My deepest gratitude to my family:

Simon,
Jean-Louis
Dominic

for their unwavering support throughout my journey of writing this book.

Nothing could be done without love.

www.ingramcontent.com/pod-product-compliance
Lightning Source LLC
Chambersburg PA
CBHW031307120726
47906CB00003B/927